RESEARCH BIBLIOGRAPHIES & CHECKLISTS

21

Marie de France: an analytical bibliography

RESEARCH BIBLIOGRAPHIES & CHECKLISTS

R*C*B

General editors

A.D. Deyermond, J.R. Little and J.E. Varey

MARIE DE FRANCE

an analytical bibliography

GLYN S. BURGESS

Grant & Cutler Ltd
1977

ISBN 0 7293 0044 7

I.S.B.N. 84-399-7933-9

DEPÓSITO LEGAL: V. 3.615 - 1977

Printed in Spain by Artes Gráficas Soler, S.A., Valencia
for

GRANT & CUTLER LTD
11, BUCKINGHAM STREET, LONDON, W. C.2.

Editors' Preface

* * *

The aim of this series is to provide research students and scholars with bibliographical information on aspects of Western European literature from the Middle Ages to the present day, in a convenient and accessible form. We hope to supplement, not to supplant, existing material. Single authors, periods or topics will be chosen for treatment wherever a gap needs to be filled and an authoritative scholar is prepared to fill it. Compilers will choose the form appropriate to each subject, ranging from the unannotated checklist to the selective critical bibliography; full descriptive bibliography is not, however, envisaged. Supplements will be issued, when appropriate, to keep the bibliographies up to date.

CONTENTS

INTRODUCTION

The following pages offer to the reader a bibliography for the three texts commonly accepted as the work of Marie de France: the twelve *lais* of MS Harley 978, the *Fables* and the *Espurgatoire Seint Patriz*. References to other works claimed for Marie by some scholars, the *Evangile aux femmes* the *Vie de Sainte Audree, Guingamor, Tydorel*, the *Lai de l'Espine*, etc., are included only where appropriate. Similarly, items concerned with topics which overlap imperceptibly with matters of direct importance to Marie – the Breton *lai*, the history of the fable, the legend of the Purgatory of St Patrick, the influence of Marie on later writers, etc. – are reduced to a minimum.

The Bibliography aims to embrace all items published before the end of 1975, which are concerned in whole or in substantial part with Marie de France. Those shorter references which I have been able to locate are also included. Anthologies are mentioned only if the text of at least one complete *lai* or fable is present and references to encyclopedias and histories of literature are confined to those in which the writer makes a useful contribution to the study of Marie de France. Entries for articles and books are accompanied by comments which attempt to act as a guide to rather than a summary of the contents. In the case of books the table of contents is normally provided as the most significant indicator of the scope of the item. Personal interventions by way of eulogy or criticism have been strictly limited and remarks for each entry aim at suggesting the degree to which it will be useful to the reader. Items accompanied by an asterisk have regrettably remained inaccessible. Titles of *lais* and quotations in the comments have been standardized in accordance with the edition of A. Ewert (item 3). Different editions of the same work are included -in a single entry except where substantial changes are involved. In the case of anthologies reference is normally made only to the most recent edition.

I should like to thank all those scholars who have provided

offprints and suggestions. For help in the preparation of the text I am particularly grateful to Dr H.S. Kay and Professor E.J. Mickel, Jr. The final stages of revision owe much to Dr I. Short, and to Professor A.D. Deyermond, whose editorial wisdom has rescued me from many inaccuracies. To those scholars whose works on Marie de France contain substantial bibliographies I should also like to record my gratitude. Without their efforts the difficult terrain over which the bibliographer journeys would have been impassable.

G.S.B.

Liverpool

February, 1977

I. MANUSCRIPTS

The *Lais*

1   H. British Library, Harley 978, ff.118a-160a (old foliation 139a-181a). Anglo-Norman, mid-thirteenth century. Contains the general prologue, the *Lais* (in the order *Guigemar, Equitan, Le Fresne, Bisclavret, Lanval, Deus Amanz, Yonec, Laüstic, Milun, Chaitivel, Chevrefoil* and *Eliduc).* See items 264 and 452.

2   S. Paris, Bibliothèque Nationale, nouv. acq. fr. 1104, ff.1a-45d. Francien, end of thirteenth century. Contains *Guigemar, Lanval, Yonec, Chevrefoil, Deus Amanz* (11. 1-159), *Bisclavret* (from 1. 233), *Milun, Le Fresne* and *Equitan.*

3   P. Bibliothèque Nationale, fr. 2168, ff.47a-58b. Picard, second half of thirteenth century. Contains *Yonec* (from 1. 396), *Guigemar* and *Lanval.*

4   C. British Library, Cott. Vesp. B. XIV, ff.1-8. Anglo-Norman, end of thirteenth century. Contains *Lanval.*

5   Q. Bibliothèque Nationale, fr. 24432, ff.241b-245a. Francien, fourteenth century. Contains *Yonec.*

The *Fables*

1   A. British Library, Harley 978, ff.40a-67b. Mid-thirteenth century.

2   B. British Library, Vesp. B. XIV, ff.19a-32b. Thirteenth century.

3   C. British Library, Harley 4333, ff.73-96. Thirteenth century.

4   D. Bodleian, Douce 132, ff.35-61b. Thirteenth-fourteenth century.

5   E. Cambridge, E.e.6.11, ff.39-83. First half of thirteenth century.

6   F. Bibliothèque Nationale, fr. 12603, ff.279c-301b. Thirteenth-fourteenth century.

7   G. Bibliothèque Nationale, fr. 4939, ff.123-44. Fifteenth-sixteenth century.

8   H. Arsenal 3142, ff.256-71. End of thirteenth century.

9   I. Bibliothèque Nationale, fr. 24310, ff.55-92. Fifteenth century.

10   K. Bibliothèque Nationale, fr. 25545, ff.29a-45d. Fourteenth century.

11   L. Bibliothèque Nationale, fr. 25406, ff.31a-49b. Thirteenth-fourteenth century.

12   M. Bibliothèque Nationale, fr. 1822, ff.198a^{bis}b. Thirteenth century.

13   N. Bibliothèque Nationale, fr. 1593, ff.47a-98d. Thirteenth century.

14   O. Bibliothèque Nationale, fr. 1446, ff.88d-108c. Thirteenth-fourteenth century.

15   P. Bibliothèque Nationale, fr. 2168, ff.159a-186b. Thirteenth century.

16   Q. Bibliothèque Nationale, fr. 2173, ff.58a-92b. Thirteenth century.

17   R. Bibliothèque Nationale, fr. 14971, ff.1-41. Fourteenth century.

18   S. Bibliothèque Nationale, fr. 19152, ff.15a-24d. Thirteenth-fourteenth century. See item 162.

19   T. Bibliothèque Nationale, fr. 24428, ff.89a-114d. Thirteenth century.

20   V. Bibliothèque Nationale, fr. 25405, ff.55c-81c. Fourteenth century.

21   W. Brussels, Bibliothèque Royale, 10296, ff.206c-230d. Fifteenth century.

22   Y. York Minster XVI, K.12, pt. I, ff.1-21d. Thirteenth-fourteenth century.

23   Z. Vatican Ottob. 3064, ff. 235-42. Fourteenth-fifteenth century.

The order in which MSS are presented here follows that of A. Ewert and R.C. Johnston (item 19, pp. xii-xiii) who have regularized alphabetically the sigla found in K. Warnke (item 22, pp. iii-xii).

The *Espurgatoire Seint Patriz*

1   Bibliothèque Nationale, fr. 25407, ff.102-22. End of thirteenth century.

II. EDITIONS, TRANSLATIONS AND ADAPTATIONS

The *Lais*
(Complete editions, and important editions of one or more *lais*)

1   Battaglia, Salvatore. *Maria di Francia, Lais: testo, versione e introduzione.* Naples: Morano (Speculum, raccolta di testi medievali e moderni, II), 1948.
     Contains a useful introduction (reprinted in *La coscienza letteraria del medioevo.* Naples: Liguori, 1965, pp. 309-59), and the text of MS H with a translation at the foot of the page. No notes or variants.

2   De Bernardi, Franca. 'Il *lai* di *Gugemer* di Maria di Francia', in *Omaggio a Camillo Guerrieri-Crocetti.* Genoa: Bozzi (Studi e Testi Romanzi e Mediolatini, II), 1971, pp. 181-250.
     Presents a new edition of *Guigemar* based on MS P with useful introductory comments on the manuscript tradition.

3   Ewert, Alfred. *Marie de France: Lais.* Oxford: Blackwell (Blackwell's French Texts), 1944.
     Good edition. Contains an introduction (pp. v-xxv), bibliography, the text of MS H, a list of rejected readings, notes, a good glossary (pp. 189-218) and an index of proper names.
     Review by:
.1   U.T. Holmes, Jr, *Speculum*, XX (1945), 114-16.

4   Harris, Julian. *Marie de France: the Lays Gugemar, Lanval and a Fragment of Yonec, with a Study of the Life and Work of the Author.* New York: Columbia University (Publications of the Institute of French Studies), 1930.
     An edition of MS P. The introduction contains sections on characterization and style, and on the originality of Marie.
     Review by:
.1   B.H.J. Weerenbeck, *Neophilologus*, XVII (1932), 152-5.

5   Hoepffner, Ernest. *Marie de France, Les Lais.* 2 vols, Strasbourg: Heitz (Bibliotheca Romanica, CCLXXIV-CCLXXV, CCLXXVII-CCLXXVIII), 1921.
     Vol. I contains *Guigemar, Lanval, Eliduc* and *Chevrefoil,* vol. II *Yonec,*

the *Deus Amanz, Bisclavret, Milun, Le Fresne, Equitan, Laüstic* and *Chaitivel.* The text is that of MS H with the orthography of MS S. Offers also a good introduction with many useful literary comments (pp. v-xxiii) and a glossary.
Review by:

.1   L. Foulet, *Romania,* XLIX (1923), 127-9.

6   Levi, Ezio. *Maria di Francia: Eliduc, riveduto nel testo, con versione a fronte, introduzione e commento.* Florence: Sansoni (Biblioteca Sansoniana Straniera, XXXIII), 1924.
A useful edition. The substantial introduction (pp. vii-xciv) makes important contributions to the story of Eliduc.
Reviews by:

.1   A. Hilka, *Zeitschrift für romanische Philologie,* XLVI (1926), 503.

.2   J.J. Salverda de Grave, *Neophilologus,* X (1925), 63-4.

.3   A. Wallensköld, *Neuphilologische Mitteilungen,* XXVI (1925), 39-41.

7   Linker, Robert W. *The Lays of Marie de France.* Chapel Hill: The Book Exchange, 1947.
A mimeographed edition with regularized spelling and a partial glossary.

8   Lods, Jeanne. *Les Lais de Marie de France.* Paris: Champion (Classiques Français du Moyen Age, LXXXVII), 1959.
Contains an introduction (pp. iii-xxxiv) with many useful literary comments and a study of the language of MS H, a bibliography (pp. xxxv-viii), the text of MS H with a list of rejected readings and variants, a short glossary and an index of proper names.
Reviews by:

.1   J. Bourciez, *Revue des Langues Romanes,* LXXIV (1960), 136-7.

.2   R. Levy, *Romance Philology,* XV (1961-2), 81-3.

.3   A.Vàrvaro, *Studi Francesi,* XII (1960), 518.

9   Mercatanti, Caterina L. 'Il *lai* di *Lanval',* in *Omaggio a Camillo Guerrieri-Crocetti.* Genoa: Bozzi (Studi e Testi Romanzi e Mediolatini, II), 1971, pp. 353-414.
Presents a new edition of *Lanval* based on MS P.

10   Neri, Ferdinando. *I Lai di Maria di Francia.* Turin: Chiantore, 1946.
Contains an introduction (pp. ix-xxx), bibliography (pp. xxxi-xxxvi), the text of MS H with a facing translation into Italian prose, notes and two appendices, 'Guigemar e Prodesaggio' (pp. 389-97, see item 338) and 'La voce *lai* nei testi italiani' (pp. 399-419).
Reviews by:

.1   A. Monteverdi, *Cultura Neolatina,* VI-VII (1946-7), 219-20.

.2   R.M. Ruggieri, *Cultura Neolatina,* VIII (1948), 139-41.

11   Richthofen, Erich von. *Vier altfranzösische Lais der Marie de France (Chievrefeuil, Äustic, Bisclavret, Guingamor).* Tübingen: Niemeyer (Sammlung romanischer Übungstexte, XXXIX), 1954; 2nd ed. 1960; 3rd ed. 1968.

Contains an introduction with an extensive bibliography (pp. v-xii) and a good glossary (pp. 43-63). Also includes a text of the Prologue.

Reviews by:

.1   R. De Cesare, *Studi Francesi,* XII (1960), 517-18.

.2   R. Guiette, *Revue Belge de Philologie et d'Histoire,* XXXV (1957), 281.

.3   M.D. Legge, *Modern Language Review,* L (1955), 572.

.4   R. Nagel, *Zeitschrift für romanische Philologie,* LXXXVII (1971), 147-8.

12   Roquefort, B. de. *Poésies de Marie de France, poète anglonormand du XIIIe siècle, ou recueil de lais, fables et autres productions de cette femme célèbre.* Paris, 2 vols, 1819-20.

Vol. I contains an introduction (pp. 1-41), the Prologue and twelve *lais,* normally attributed to Marie, and two other *lais, Graelent* and the *Lai de l'Espine.* Vol. II contains a *Notice sur les Fables* (pp. i-lviii), 103 Fables, a *Notice sur le Purgatoire de Saint-Patrice* (pp. 403-10) and the text of the *Espurgatoire.* The *Lais* are accompanied by a translation into Modern French.

Review by:

.1   F.J.M. Raynouard, *Journal des Savants* (1820), 395-404 and 451-60.

13   Rychner, Jean. *Les Lais de Marie de France.* Paris: Champion (Classiques Français du Moyen Age, XCIII), 1966.

Excellent edition. Contains an introduction (pp. vii-xxviii), a lengthy bibliography (pp. xxviii-xlv), the text of MS H, a list of rejected readings and variants, useful notes, an index of proper names and a good glossary (pp. 293-317).

Reviews by:

.1   R. De Cesare, *Studi Francesi,* XXX (1966), 528-9.

.2   A. Ewert, *French Studies,* XXII (1968), 52-4.

.3   E. A. Francis, *Medium Aevum,* XXXVII (1968), 195-6.

.4   J. Frappier, *Romance Philology,* XXII (1968-9), 600-13 (see item 191).

.5   W. Günther, *Neue Züricher Zeitung,* no. 175 (15 Jan., 1967).

.6   H. Guiter, *Revue des Langues Romanes,* LXXVII bis (1967), 262-3.

.7   R. Nagel, *Zeitschrift für romanische Philologie,* LXXXV (1969), 277-81.

.8   C. Segre, *Cahiers de Civilisation Médiévale,* XI (1968), 243-6.

.9   A. Stefenelli, *Vox Romanica,* XXVIII (1969), 162-4.

14   Rychner, Jean and Paul Aebischer. *Marie de France, Le Lai de Lanval,* texte critique et édition diplomatique des quatre manuscrits français, accompagné du texte du *Ianuals ljoð et de*

sa traduction française, avec une introduction et des notes.
Geneva: Droz (Textes Littéraires Français), 1958.
Text by Rychner, introduction and notes by Aebischer.
Reviews by:

.1   A. Ewert, *Romance Philology,* XIII (1959-60), 178-80.

.2   E. A. Francis, *French Studies,* XIV (1960), 63-4.

.3   J. Harris, *Romanic Review,* LI (1960), 219-20.

.4   O. Jodogne, *Les Lettres Romanes,* XIV (1960), 279-81.

.5   J. Lods, *Romania,* LXXIX (1958), 425-8.

.6   J. Monfrin, *Bibliothèque de l'Ecole des Chartes,* CXIX (1961), 297.

.7   R. C. D. Perman, *Modern Language Review,* LIV (1959), 110-11.

.8   G. Raynaud de Lage, *Le Moyen Age,* LXV (1959), 617-18.

15   Warnke, Karl. *Die Lais der Marie de France,* mit vergleichenden Anmerkungen von Reinhold Köhler. lst ed.,Halle: Niemeyer (Bibliotheca Normannica, III), 1885, 276pp.
An excellent edition. Contains an introduction (pp. iii-lv) including a lengthy section on Marie's language, R. Köhler's useful comments on each *lai* (pp. lix-cviii), the text of MS H with rejected readings and variants at the foot of the page, notes, a good glossary (pp. 231-74) and a list of proper names.
Reviews by:

.1   C. Chabaneau, *Revue des Langues Romanes,* 4th series, II (1888), 217.

.2   A. Mussafia, *Literaturblatt für germanische und romanische Philologie,* VI (1885), cols 497-502.

.3   G. Paris, *Romania,* XIV (1885), 598-608.

.4   A. Tobler, *Zeitschrift für romanische Philologie,* X (1886), 164-9 (see item 440).

.5   M. Wilmotte, *Revue de l'Instruction Publique (Supérieure et Moyenne) en Belgique,* XXX (1887), 47-9.

16   — , *Die Lais der Marie de France,* mit vergleichenden Anmerkungen von Reinhold Köhler. 2nd ed., Halle: Niemeyer (Bibliotheca Normannica, III), 1900, 303 pp.
Contains expanded introduction and glossary (pp. 299-301).
Review by:

.1   G. Cohn, *Zeitschrift für französische Sprache und Literatur,* XXIV (1902), 11-73.

17   — , *Die Lais der Marie de France,* mit vergleichenden Anmerkungen von Reinhold Köhler, nebst Ergänzungen von Johannes Bolte und einem Anhang von Peter Kusel. 3rd ed., Halle: Niemeyer (Bibliotheca Normannica, III), 1925, 344pp. Reprint, Geneva: Slatkine, 1974.
Adds to item 16 a section on Foulet's theories (pp. xlvi-lx) and the text

of *Guingamor.*

Reviews by:

.1 E. Brugger, *Zeitschrift für französische Sprache und Literatur,* XLIX (1926), 116-55 (see item 109).

.2 E. Hoepffner, *Neophilologus,* XI (1926), 141-50.

.3 H. F. Muller, *Romanic Review,* XVI (1925), 95-7.

.4 W. A. Nitze, *Modern Philology,* XXIII (1925-6), 233.

.5 O. Schultz-Gora, *Zeitschrift für romanische Philologie,* XLVI (1926) 314-25 (see item 410).

18 —, *Vier Lais der Marie de France,* nach der Handschrift des Mus. Brit. Harl. 978 mit Einleitung und Glossar. Halle: Niemeyer (Sammlung romanischer Übungstexte, II), 1925.

Contains *Bisclavret, Chevrefoil, Lanval, Laüstic* and the Prologue.

The *Fables*
(Complete editions and important selections)

19 Ewert, Alfred and Ronald C. Johnston. *Marie de France: Fables.* Oxford: Blackwell (Blackwell's French Texts), 1942.

Contains an introduction (pp. v-xx), the Prologue to the *Fables,* 46 fables based on MS Harley 978, and the Epilogue. Notes and a glossary are also provided.

20 Gumbrecht, Hans U. *Marie de France: Äsop, eingeleitet, kommentiert und übersetzt.* Munich: Fink (Klassische Texte des romanischen Mittelalters in zweisprachigen Ausgaben, XII), 1973. For comment, see Addenda, p. 111.

Review by:

.1 K. Baldinger, *Zeitschrift für romanische Philologie,* LXXXIX (1973), 699.

21 Warnke, Karl. *Aus dem Esope der Marie de France: eine Auswahl von dreissig Stücken,* lst ed., Halle: Niemeyer (Sammlung romanische Übungstexte, IX), 1926; 2nd ed., Tübingen: Niemeyer, 1962.

Contains an introduction (pp. vii-xii) and a glossary (pp. 49-61).

22 —, *Die Fabeln der Marie de France,* mit Benutzung des von Ed. Mall hinterlassenen Materials. Halle: Niemeyer (Bibliotheca Normannica, VI), 1898. Reprint, Geneva: Slatkine, 1974.

A substantial introduction (pp. iii-cxlvi) is followed by the Prologue to the *Fables,* the text of 102 fables with variants, the Epilogue, appendices, notes, an excellent glossary, a list of proper names and folio references for the location of each fable in the manuscripts.

* * *

For editions not listed in this section see items 12, 27, 33, 55, 56, 57 and 437.

The *Espurgatoire Seint Patriz*

23   *Farcy de Pontfarcy, Yolande de. *L'Espurgatoire Seint Patriz*. Thèse de IIIe cycle (unpublished), University of Rennes II, 1971.

24   Jenkins, Thomas A. *Marie de France: Espurgatoire Seint Patriz, an Old French Poem of the Twelfth Century published with an Introduction and a Study of the Language of the Author*. Philadelphia, 1894. Reprint, Geneva: Slatkine, 1974.

Contains an introduction (pp. 1-16), a description of the MS (pp. 17-20), remarks on the dialect of Marie de France (pp. 21-8) and on the language of the *Espurgatoire* (pp. 29-50), the text with rejected readings and notes. No glossary. See item 25.
Reviews by:

.1   G. Paris, *Romania,* XXIV (1895), 290-5.

.2   K. Warnke, *Literaturblatt für germanische und romanische Philologie,* XVI (1895), cols 82-7.

25   — , *The Espurgatoire Seint Patriz of Marie de France, with a Text of the Latin Original.* Chicago: University of Chicago Press (Decennial Publications, VII), 1903.

A 2nd ed. of item 24; adds a text of the *Tractatus* of Henry of Saltrey (British Library, MS Harley 3846).
Reviews by:

.1   G. Cohn, *Literaturblatt für germanische und romanische Philologie,* XXVI (1905), cols 280-94.

.2   L.M. Gay, *Modern Language Notes,* XVIII (1903), 247-8.

26   Warnke, Karl. *Das Buch vom Espurgatoire S. Patrice der Marie de France und seine Quelle.* Halle: Niemeyer (Bibliotheca Normannica, IX), 1938.

Contains an introduction (pp. iii-lii), the text of the *Espurgatoire* facing two versions of the *Tractatus* of Henry of Saltrey, and a short glossary (pp. 175-8).

Review by:

.1   K. Voretzsch, *Archiv für das Studium der neueren Sprachen und Literaturen,* CLXXV (1939), 111-20.

* * *

For the edition of the *Espurgatoire* by B. de Roquefort, see item 12.

Anthologies and other editions of a complete *lai* or fable.

27   Auguis, P.R. *Les Poètes françois depuis le XIIe siècle jusqu'à Malherbe, avec une notice historique et littéraire sur chaque poète.* 6 vols, Paris: Crapelet, 1824.
> Marie is the subject of pp. 410-47. An introduction, in which Marie is seen as a thirteenth-century poet with the *Lais* dedicated to Henry III and the *Fables* to William Longsword, is followed by the text of *Graelent* and six fables (ed. Warnke, nos. I, II, III, V, VII, XXXIX).

28   Bartsch, Karl. *La Langue et la littérature françaises depuis le IXème siècle jusqu'au XIVème siècle:* textes et glossaire précédés d'une grammaire de l'ancien français par Adolf Horning. Paris: Maisonneuve & Ch. Leclerc, 1887.
> Contains a complete text of *Bisclavret,* edited by H. Suchier, cols 271-8, and two fables, *De catto infatulato* (ed. Warnke, no. CL) and *De femina et gallina* (ed. Warnke, no. CII), cols 277-80.

29   Bartsch, Karl and Leo Wiese. *Chrestomathie de l'ancien français (VIIIe - XVe siècles), accompagnée d'une grammaire et d'un glossaire.* 12th ed., Leipzig: Vogel, 1919. Reprint, New York: Hafner, 1958.
> Contains a complete text of *Laüstic,* the Prologue to the *Fables* and three fables (ed. Warnke, nos I, II, XXV).

30   *Erling, Ludwig. *Li Lais de Lanval, altfranzösisches Gedicht der Marie de France, nebst Th. Chestre's Launfal.* Kempten: (Programm der K. bayerischen Studienanstalt zu Kempten für das Schuljahr 1882-3), 1883.

31   Groult, P., V. Emond and G. Muraille. *Anthologie de la littérature française du moyen âge.* 2 vols, 3rd ed., Gembloux: Duculot, 1964.
> Contains a complete text of *Laüstic* (vol. I, pp. 119-24) with notes (vol. II, pp. 66-70) and the fable *De lupo et agno* (ed. Warnke, no. II), vol. I, pp. 163-4.

32   Henry, Albert. *Chrestomathie de la littérature en ancien français.* 2nd ed., Berne: Francke (Bibliotheca Romanica, Scripta Romanica Selecta, III), 1960.
Contains a complete text of *Laüstic* and two fables, *De vidua* and *Iterum de muliere et proco eius* (ed. Warnke, nos XXV and XLV).

33   Ideler, Julius L. *Geschichte der altfranzösischen National-Literatur von den ersten Anfängen bis auf Franz I.* Berlin, 1842.
Contains a text of the *Deus Amanz* (Section B, pp. 25-33) and four fables (*ibid.,* pp. 33-6, ed. Warnke, nos. XI, XIII, XIV, XXXIII).

34   Michel, Francisque. *Tristan: recueil de ce qui reste des poëmes relatifs à ses aventures composés en françois, en anglo-normand et en grec dans les XII et XIII siècles.* 3 vols, London: Pickering; Paris: Techener, 1835-9.
Vol. II (1835) contains a text of *Chevrefoil* (pp. 139-46).

35   Mölk, Ulrich. *Französische Literarästhetik des 12. und 13. Jahrhunderts: Prologe - Exkurse -Epiloge.* Tübingen: Niemeyer (Sammlung romanischer Übungstexte, LIV), 1969.
Contains the general prologue to the *Lais* (pp. 66-7), the prologue to the *Fables* (pp. 69-71) and the epilogue to the *Fables* (p. 71).

36   Palfrey, Thomas R. and William C. Holbrook. *Medieval French Literature: Representative Selections in Modernized Versions.* New York: Appleton-Century-Crofts (The Century Modern Language Series), 1934.
Modernized text of *Chevrefoil* and extracts from *Lanval* (pp. 95-106).

37   Pauphilet, Albert. *Poètes et romanciers du moyen âge.* Paris: Gallimard (Bibliothèque de la Pléiade), 1939.
Contains complete texts of *Guigemar, Lanval, Chevrefoil* and *Laüstic* (pp. 297-345).

38   Payen, Jean C. *Les Tristan en vers: Tristan de Béroul, Tristan de Thomas, Folie Tristan de Berne, Folie Tristan d'Oxford, Chèvrefeuille de Marie de France.* Edition nouvelle comprenant texte, traduction, notes critiques, bibliographie et notes. Paris: Garnier, 1974.
The text and translation of *Chevrefoil* are found on pp. 299-302.

39   Pottier, Bernard. *Textes médiévaux français et romans: des gloses latines à la fin du XVe siècle.* Paris: Klincksieck, 1964.
Contains a complete text of *Chevrefoil* (pp. 67-9).

40   Roncaglia, Aurelio. *Antologia delle letterature medievali d'oc e d'oïl* Milan: Edizioni Accademia, 1961; 2nd ed., 1973.

Contains the text and a translation into Italian of *Laüstic* (1st ed., pp. 472-82; 2nd ed., pp. 466-75).

41   Studer, Paul and E.G.R. Waters. *Historical French Reader: Medieval Period.* Oxford: Clarendon Press, 1924, etc.

Contains a complete text of the *Deus Amanz* (pp. 88-97).

42   Voretzsch, Karl. *Altfranzösisches Lesebuch.* 3rd ed., Tübingen: Niemeyer, 1966.

Contains a complete text of *Bisclavret* (pp. 131-5) and two fables, *De corvo et vulpe* and *De vulpe et ursa* (ed. Warnke, nos XIII and LXIX), pp. 70-1.

Translations and Adaptations

43   **Arcydzieła francuskiego Średniowiecza.* Warsaw: Państwowy Instytut Wydawniczy (State Publishing Institute), 1968.

Contains a translation of ten of Marie's *lais* by Anna Tatarkiewicz.

44   Cohen, Gustave. *Anthologie de la littérature française du moyen-âge.* Paris: Delagrave, 1946.

Contains a complete translation of the *Deus Amanz* (pp. 52-9). See items 127 and 128.

45   Costello, Louisa S. *Specimens of the Early Poetry of France from the Time of the Troubadours and Trouvères to the Reign of Henri Quatre.* London: Pickering, 1835.

Contains a free verse rendering of *Bisclavret* (pp. 50-61) and *Chevrefoil* (pp. 61-7). Introduction (pp. 43-9) summarizes earlier theories relating to Marie.

46   Ellis, George. *Specimens of Early English Metrical Romances.* 3 vols, London, 1805.

English paraphrase of the *Lais,* with the exception of *Guigemar, Lanval* and *Chevrefoil* (vol. I, pp. 137-90).

46a   —, *Specimens of Early English Metrical Romances.* 2nd ed., revised by J.O. Halliwell. 1 vol. London: Bohn (Bohn's Antiquarian Library), 1848, pp. 45-74 and 538-46.

47 Fowles, John. *The Ebony Tower.* London: Cape, 1974.
Contains a translation of *Eliduc* with an interesting introductory note (pp. 117-41).

48 Frappier, Jean. *Les Romans courtois.* Paris: Classiques Larousse, 1943.
Contains an adaptation of *Guigemar* with extracts from the Old French text (pp. 37-49) and a translation of *Chevrefoil* (pp. 49-51) and *Laüstic* (pp. 51-3).

49 Hertz, Wilhelm. *Marie de France: poetische Erzählungen nach altbretonischen Liebes-Sagen.* Stuttgart, 1862.
Contains an introduction, the Prologue (said to be for Henry III of England) and ten of the *Lais*. Summaries of *Laüstic* and *Chaitivel* are added in the Appendix.

50 —, *Spielmannsbuch: Novellen in Versen aus dem 12. und 13. Jahrhundert, übertragen.* 3rd ed., Stuttgart and Berlin, 1905. Reprint, Walhuf bei Wiesbaden: Martin Sändig, n.d.
Contains translations into German verse of *Lanval, Yonec, Deus Amanz, Le Fresne,* and *Eliduc.* Very useful notes.

51 Jonin, Pierre. *Les Lais de Marie de France,* traduits de l'ancien français Paris: Champion, 1972.
The best available translation. The introduction contains interesting remarks on the difficulties of translating an Old French text.

52 Koulakovski, S. *Trois lais de Marie de France traduits en russe.* St Petersburg and Leipzig, 1923.
Translation of *Bisclavret, Laüstic* and *Chevrefoil.*

53 Lancaster, Charles M. *Saints and Sinners in Old Romance: Poems of Feudal France and England.* Nashville: Vanderbilt University Press, 1941. Reprint, New York: Russell and Russell, 1971.
Contains a verse translation of *Chevrefoil* (pp. 199-203).

54 Lebesgue, Philéas. *Six lais d'amour modernisés.* Paris: Sansot, 1913.
Contains *Lanval, Chevrefoil, Eliduc, Guigemar, Laüstic* and *Yonec.*

55 Legrand d'Aussy, Pierre-Jean-Baptiste. *Fabliaux ou contes du XIIe et du XIIIe siècle.* 4 vols, Paris, 1779.
Contains a Modern French version of *Lanval* (vol. I, pp. 93-105, notes pp. 105-19), an extract in Modern French from *Guigemar* (vol. III, pp. 251-8) and forty-three fables (vol. IV, pp. 169-248) in a translation

based on four MSS. Marie, who is presented as living around the middle of the thirteenth century (vol. III, p. 441, see Baum, item 85, p. 65), is not named as the author of the *lais*. See items 56, 57 and 69.

56 —, *Fabliaux ou contes, du XIIe et du XIIIe siècle, fables et roman du XIIIe.* 5 vols, 2nd ed., Paris, 1781.

Contains, in addition to the items in the first edition (*Lanval,* vol. I, pp. 92-124; *Guigemar,* vol. IV, pp. 110-18; fables, vol. IV, pp. 319-421), a summary of the *Espurgatoire* (vol. V, pp. 130-4) and some general remarks on Marie (vol. IV, pp. 321-36). The count to whom the *Fables* were dedicated is seen as Guillaume de Dampierre. See items 55, 57 and 69.

57 —, *Fabliaux ou contes, fables et romans du XIIe et du XIIIe siècle.* 5 vols, 3rd ed., Paris, 1829. Reprint, Geneva: Slatkine, 1971.

Adds to the material contained in the second edition (*Lanval,* vol. I, pp. 165-94; *Guigemar,* vol. IV, pp. 150-6; fables, vol. IV, pp. 321-400, *Espurgatoire,* vol. V, pp. 93-9) only the text in Old French of the fable of the Eagle and the Hawk (vol. IV, appendix, p. 30, ed. Warnke, no. LXII). The *Lai de l'Espine* (vol. IV, pp. 144-9, appendix, pp. 10-13) and *Graelent* (vol. I, pp. 195-207, appendix, pp. 16-23) also occur under Marie's name. See items 55, 56 and 69.

58 Luquiens, F.B. *Three Lays of Marie de France retold in English Verse.* New York: Holt, 1911.

Abridged renderings in blank verse of *Lanval, Le Fresne* and the *Deus Amanz.*

59 Mason, Eugene. *French Mediaeval Romances from the Lays of Marie de France.* London: Dent; New York: Dutton (Everyman's Library), 1911. Reprinted in 1954 under the title *Lays of Marie de France and other French Legends,* with a note by E.A. Francis.

Reviews of reprint by:
.1 A. Ewert, *French Studies,* VIII (1954), 383.
.2 J.H. Watkins, *Medium Aevum,* XXIV (1955), 68-9.

60 —, *Old-World Love Stories from the Lays of Marie de France and other Mediaeval Romances and Legends,* illustrated and decorated by Reginald L. Knowles. London: Dent; New York: Dutton, 1913.

Contains all the *Lais* with the exception of *Equitan.* Does not translate the Prologue.

61 Moréas, Jean. *Contes de la vieille France.* Paris: Mercure de France, 1904, etc.
Contains adaptations of *Eliduc, Guigemar, Yonec, Chevrefoil* and *Le Fresne.* See item 202.

62 O'Shaughnessy, Arthur W.E. *Lays of France, founded on the Lays of Marie.* London: Ellis-Green, 1872; 2nd ed., London: Chatto and Windus, 1874.
Adaptations in verse of *Laüstic,* the *Deus Amanz, Chaitivel, Eliduc* and *Yonec.* Little resemblance to Marie's text.

63 Reeves, James. *The Shadow of the Hawk.* London: Collins, 1975.
Six of Marie's *lais (Yonec, Lanval, Laüstic, Bisclavret, Le Fresne* and *Guigemar)* are adapted for children.

64 Rickert, Edith. *Marie de France: Seven of her Lays done into English,* with designs by Caroline Watt. Long Acre: Nutt, 1901.
Translations of *Guigemar, Le Fresne,* the *Deus Amanz, Yonec, Laüstic, Chevrefoil* and *Eliduc.* Contains an introduction (pp. 137-64) and notes.

65 St. Clair, Foster Y. 'Marie de France, *Le Chaitivel:* Translation and Commentary', *Proceedings of the Linguistic Circle of Manitoba and North Dakota,* X (1970), 5-10.
The translation, part prose, part verse, is followed by some general remarks on Marie and *Le Chaitivel.*

66 Terry, Patricia. *Lays of Courtly Love in Verse Translation.* Introduction by Charles W. Dunn. New York: Doubleday, 1963.
General introduction to Marie, pp. xi-xiii. Translations of *Laüstic, Chevrefoil,* the *Deus Amanz* and *Eliduc.*

67 Tuffrau, Paul. *Les Lais de Marie de France,* transposés en français moderne. Paris: Piazza, 1923.
Does not translate *Equitan* or *Chaitivel.* Preface, pp. i-xi.

68 Voyer d'Argenson, Marc-Antoine-René de, marquis de Paulmy. *Mélanges tirés d'une grande bibliothèque.* 70 vols, Paris: Moutard, 1779-88.
Vol. XIX (1781) mentions Marie de France and offers the first ten lines of the Prologue to the *Fables* and a translation of five fables. See Baum, item 85, p. 64.

69   Way, G.L. *Fabliaux or Tales, abridged from French Manuscripts of the XIIth and XIIIth Centuries by M. Le Grand, selected and translated into English verse, with a Preface, Notes and Appendix by the late G. Ellis, Esq.* 3 vols, London, 1800; new ed. corrected, 1815. See items 55, 56 and 57.

        Contains a verse rendering of *Lanval* (vol. II, pp. 51-72, notes pp. 221-35) and *Guigemar* (vol. II, pp. 101-16, notes, pp. 237-46).

70   Weston, Jessie L. *Guingamor, Lanval, Tyolet, Bisclavret: Four Lais rendered into English Prose from the French of Marie de France and Others,* with designs by Caroline Watt. Long Acre: Nutt, 1900.

71   Williams, Harry F. *Les Lais de Marie de France.* Englewood Cliffs, New Jersey: Prentice-Hall, 1970.

        Translates the *Lais* into Modern French. Does not include the Prologue. Reviews by:

  .1   B.J.M. Angles, *Modern Language Journal,* LV (1971), 126-7.

  .2   W.W. Kibler, *French Review,* XLIV (1970-1), 161-3.

* * *

For translations not listed in this section see items 1, 6, 10, 12, 20, 36, 38, 40, 94, 118, 158, 290, 295, 299, 370, 395, 435, 445, 510, 511, 512, 513, 514 and 515.

III. BOOKS AND ARTICLES

Items are listed here alphabetically. A small number of cross references are provided where appropriate. For a more extensive breakdown of material relating to the *Lais*, the *Fables* and the *Espurgatoire Seint Patriz*, see the Index of Marie de France's works, pp. 115-23. The following books are devoted in their entirety to Marie de France and associated problems: items 76, 77, 78, 85, 149, 151, 158, 221, 256, 268, 316, 331, 356, 380, 390, 401, 453 and 475.

* * * * *

72   Abercrombie, Nigel. 'A Note on a Passage in *Guigemar'*,
        Modern Language Review, XXX (1935), 353.
        The expression *a l'uevre Salemon* in l. 172 of *Guigemar* indicates the
        source of Marie's description of the magic ship, i.e., Song of Songs, III,
        vv. 9-10 (Vulgate). Other passages in the Song are recalled by details in
        the description. See items 81, 114, 284 and 466.

73   Adams, Alison and T.D. Hemming. *'Chèvrefeuille* and the
        Evolution of the Tristan Legend', *Bibliographical Bulletin of
        the International Arthurian Society*, XXVIII (1976), 204-13.
        Chevrefoil contains sufficient details for us to be able to reconstruct the
        primitive version of the Tristan legend known to Marie. This version,
        which Adams and Hemming label A, did not include a second Iseut,
        had no Breton element and ended violently. It thus differed markedly
        from version B (in effect, the extant *Estoire*), to which Eilhart and
        Thomas adhere fairly faithfully. The *Prose* Tristan and Béroul, by con-
        trast, seem to draw on both A and B. Thus a close analysis of *Chevre-
        foil* suggests that the authoritative position of version B in the Tristan
        legend can no longer be maintained.

74   Adler, Alfred. 'Höfische Dialektik im *Lai du Freisne'*,
        Germanisch-romanische Monatsschrift, XLII (1961),
        44-51.
        When Le Fresne is left as a child in the tree with the rich possessions
        deriving from and anticipating her courtly status, and when she abases
        herself by offering up the rich cloth, there is a dialectic between court-
        liness and childish innocence. Contains some useful remarks on the
        concept of courtliness, seen variously as pride, rationality, social status,
        concern for external appearances, the need for secrecy in love and
        richness or splendour.

75   —, 'Structural Uses of the Fairy Mistress Theme in
        Certain *Lais* of Marie de France', *Bibliographical
        Bulletin of the International Arthurian Society*, IX
        (1957), 127-8.
        Summary of a communication presented to the Fifth Triennial Congress,
        Bangor, August, 1957. Lanval is a passive adolescent offered motherly
        protection by his fairy mistress. In *Le Fresne* the heroine functions like
        a fairy mistress, acting with Christian *humilitas* and effecting a magic
        transformation. Eliduc's wife is a model Christian and fairy mistress
        combined.

76   Ahlström, Axel. *Marie de France et les lais narratifs*. Gothen-
        burg (Göteborgs Kungl. Vetenskaps=och Vitterhets=Samhälles
        Handlingar, fjärde Földjen, vol. XXIX, iii), 1925, 34pp.
        Still a useful study. Contains three chapters: (1)'Quand les lais narratifs
        furent-ils écrits?', (2) 'Les opinions récentes de l'origine des lais',
        (3)'La personne et l'oeuvre de Marie'. Marie is seen as a highly cultivated
        woman who knew Latin and English and was thoroughly acquainted
        with the life and customs of the feudal châteaux. She was possibly of
        noble birth and had close relations with William of Gloucester to whom
        she probably dedicated the *Fables*. The *Lais* must have been composed
        during the period 1160-5. But Marie was not a great author and owes
        the entire contents of her poems to her sources. The modifications she
        made to her sources merely produced banality.

77   —, *Studier i den fornfranska Lais-Litteraturen*. Uppsala:
        Almquist, 1892, xvi + 168pp.
        A wide-ranging and useful study containing comments on each of
        Marie's *lais* and a discussion of issues such as the etymology of the term
        lai, the meaning of the terms *breton* and *Bretagne,* the origin of the
        lais bretons and the way in which Breton *lais* became narrative *lais*.
        Studies the geographical references in each *lai* and accepts H.Zimmer's

opinion (items 480 and 481) concerning the origin of the *lais*.
Review by:

.1   G. Paris, *Romania,* XXIV (1895), 528.

78   Baader, Horst. *Die Lais: zur Geschichte einer Gattung der altfranzösischen Kurzerzählungen.* Frankfurt: Klostermann (Analecta Romanica, XVI), 1966.
An important and wide-ranging study. Chapter headings are (1) *Lai.* Der Name und seine Bedeutungen, (2) Die Quellen der erzählenden *Lais* nach deren eigenem Zeugnis, (3) Die Herkunft der *aventures,* (4) Die *Lais* und die Volksmärchen, (5) Die *Lais* als Kunstmärchen, (6) Die Lais ausserhalb Frankreichs, (7) Die schriftliche Überlieferung der altfranzösischen *Lais,* (8) Die Chronologie der *Lais,* (9) Der historische Wandel der *Lais* als Gattung, (10) Die Lais und die erzählende Literatur des französischen Mittelalters. Excellent bibliography. See Renzi, item 375.
Review by:

.1   P. Schon, *Romanische Forschungen,* LXXIX (1967), 181-4.

79   Bambeck, Manfred. 'Das Werwolfmotiv im *Bisclavret',* *Zeitschrift für romanische Philologie,* LXXXIX (1973), 123-47.
The werewolf theme was part of contemporary actuality around the middle of the twelfth century. It appears also in a tale from Giraldus Cambrensis' *Topographia hibernica,* dedicated to Henry II in 1188. Marie has minimized and humanized the originally Breton motif and made it a central element in the relationship between individuals. The king performs in *Bisclavret* the same function as Saviour that is performed by the priest in Giraldus. Contains frequent references to Battaglia, item 84.

80   —, 'Die Wieselepisode im *Eliduc* der Marie de France', *Archiv für das Studium der neueren Sprachen und Literaturen,* CCVIII (1971-2), 334-49.
The remarks of editors concerning the weasel as a folklore motif are discussed and expanded. In medieval art the weasel is a symbol of Christ and its presence in *Eliduc* lends support to Spitzer's view (item 424, p. 89) that Marie is an 'anima naturaliter christiana'.

81   Bar, F. 'Sur le texte des *Lais* de Marie de France', *Le Moyen Age,* LXVIII (1962), 153-60.
The following passages are discussed with particular reference to the readings offered by Jeanne Lods, E. Hoepffner and A. Ewert: Prologue, 26; *Guigemar,* 142, 172, 189, 333, 555, 567, 569, 579-80, 629, 638, 748, 829-30; *Lanval,* 136-7, 288, 420; *Laüstic,* 35; *Eliduc,* 21, 64-5,

129-31, 157-60, 174, 197, 209, 467-9. The article also includes a study entitled *'Oeuvre Salomon* et Nef de Salomon' (pp. 157-60).
Review by:

.1 R. De Cesare, *Studi Francesi,* XX (1963), 323.

82 Basset, René. 'La Légende du mari aux deux femmes', *Revue des Traditions Populaires,* XVI (1901), 614-16.
Adds to the examples quoted by G. Paris (item 350) a Prussian parallel and a reference to two tales from the *Arabian Nights.*

83 Battaglia, Salvatore. 'Maria di Francia', in *Enciclopedia italiana di scienze, lettere ed arti,* XII (1934), p. 294.
Useful introduction.

84 —, 'Il mito del Licantropo nel *Bisclavret* di Maria di Francia', *Filologia Romanza,* III (1956), 229-53. Reprinted in *La coscienza letteraria del medioevo.* Naples: Liguori, 1965, pp. 361-89.
A dense and useful study of the structure and meaning of *Bisclavret* with special emphasis on the fusion of two stories, the werewolf myth (found in Pliny the Elder and Petronius, etc.) and the legend of the faithful dog (attested in Pliny, Isidore of Seville, etc.). Marie has humanized the two legends and abolished the frontier between myth and real life, between rational and non-rational experience. See item 79.
Review by:

.1 R. De Cesare, *Studi Francesi,* II (1957), 288.

85 Baum, Richard, *Recherches sur les oeuvres attribuées à Marie de France.* Heidelberg: Winter (Annales Universitatis Saraviensis, Reihe: Philosophische Fakultät, IX), 1968, 241pp.
Important study. Contains abundant documentation relating to biographical and historical problems surrounding Marie and her works. Calls into question the attribution to Marie de France of the entire Harley collection, the *Fables* and the *Espurgatoire.* Only the *Fables* belong indubitably to Marie de France and there is no evidence that all the *lais* in Harley 978 were composed by the same poet.
Reviews by:

.1 F. Beggiato, *Cultura Neolatina,* XXXII (1972), 312.
.2 K. Brightenback, *Romance Philology,* XXIX (1975-6), 552-5.
.3 G. Di Stefano, *Studi Francesi,* XXXVIII (1969), 321-2.
.4 C. Leube, *Germanisch-romanische Monatsschrift,* XXII (1972), 452-5.
.5 J. Lods, *Cahiers de Civilisation Médiévale,* XIV (1971), 355-8.
.6 F. Lyons, *French Studies,* XXV (1971), 315.
.7 D.J.A. Ross, *Modern Language Review,* LXV (1970), 896-8.

.8   J. Rychner, *Vox Romanica*, XXXI (1972), 177-80.

.9   M.J.J. Spoor, *Rapports*, XLIV (1974), 105-8.

86   —, 'Les Troubadours et les lais', *Zeitschrift für romanische Philologie*, LXXXV (1969), 1-44.

An examination of the term *lais* in Provençal. This word, which has a vast and varied conceptual field, probably derives from a Latin expression.

87   Bayrav, Süheylâ. *Symbolisme médiéval: Béroul, Marie, Chrétien*. Paris: Presses Universitaires de France, and Istanbul: Maatbasi, 1957.

The *Lais* are discussed on pp. 63-72. Remarks for the most part superficial.

88   Becker, Philip A. 'Von den Erzählern neben und nach Chrestien de Troyes, V. Die Kurzerzählung in Reimpaaren', *Zeitschrift für romanische Philologie*, LVI (1936), 241-74.

Marie is the subject of pp. 252-63.

89   Bédier, Joseph. 'Les *Lais* de Marie de France', *Revue des Deux Mondes*, CVII (Sept. - Oct. 1891), 835-63. German translation in *Der arthurische Roman*, ed. Kurt Wais. Darmstadt: Wissenschaftliche Buchgesellschaft (Wege der Forschung, CLVII), 1970, pp. 56-93.

An important discussion of a number of issues relevant to Marie, her identity, the origin of the *lais,* their transmission, their literary value and relationship to the courtly romance. Bédier accepts that Marie was Norman, that she lived in England, wrote about 1175, dedicated her *Lais* to Henry II and the *Fables* probably to William Longsword. She heard the *lais* on both Breton and Celtic lips, and they were half sung, half recited, often in a garbled language. Their contribution to literature lies principally in the particular conception of love and the presence of the marvellous. The Round Table romances are derived from *lais* and are inferior to them in structure and inspiration.

90   Bertoni, G. *Studi su vecchie e nuove poesie e prose d'amore e di romanzi.* Modena: Orlandini, 1921.

Contains a chapter on Marie (pp. 55-77). General remarks.

91   Betham, Matilda. *The Lay of Marie: a Poem.* London, 1816.

Contains (pp. 157-82) a lengthy extract from the article by La Rue, item 279.

92 Beyer, Jürgen. *Schwank und Moral: Untersuchungen zum altfranzösischen Fabliau und verwandten Formen.* Heidelberg: Winter (Studia Romanica, XVI), 1968.
Chapter II is entitled 'Die Schwank-Fabeln im *Esope* der Marie de France' (pp. 34-50).

93 Bezzola, Reto R. *Les Origines et la formation de la littérature courtoise en occident (500-1200).* 3 vols, Paris: Champion (Bibliothèque de l'Ecole des Hautes Etudes: IVe section, Sciences historiques et philologiques), 1958-63.
Contains numerous references to Marie, esp. Vol. III, part 1, pp. 302-6.

94 *Bianchini, Angela. *Romanzi medievali d'amore e d'avventura.* Rome: Casini, 1957.
Contains a translation of the *Deus Amanz* (pp. 363-72).

95 Biller, Gunnar. *Etude sur le style des premiers romans français en vers (1150-75).* Gothenburg: Wettergren & Kerber (Göteborgs Högskolas Årsschrift, IV), 1916. Reprint, Geneva: Slatkine, 1974.
Contains frequent references to rhetorical figures in Marie's works.

96 Bliss, A.J. 'The Hero's Name in the Middle English Versions of *Lanval*', *Medium Aevum*, XXVII (1958), 80-5.
Includes a discussion of the name Lanval.

97 — (ed.). *Sir Launfal.* London and Edinburgh: Nelson's Medieval and Renaissance Library, 1960.
Introduction contains useful remarks on *Lanval*. Text of *Lanval*, pp. 105-28.

98 Blondheim, D.S. 'A Note on the Sources of Marie de France', *Modern Language Notes*, XXIII (1908), 201-2.
Discussion of the importance of the collection of fables entitled *Ex Romulo Nilantii ortae fabulae metricae,* which 'presents in a number of cases a form of the version of Romulus Nilantii, from which a large portion of the fables of Marie are ultimately derived, intermediate between the Nilantine original and the modified type represented by Marie'.

99 Boiron, Françoise and Jean-Charles Payen. 'Structure et sens du *Bel Inconnu* de Renaut de Beaujeu', *Le Moyen Age*, LXXVI (1970), 15-26.
Le Bel Inconnu has been influenced by *Lanval* (pp. 21-2), but the *roman d'aventure* is more optimistic, as the hero accepts his destiny as an individual in society. In *Lanval* the hero leaves behind him the world of men, 'la terre de l'épreuve et du malheur'.

100 Bosquet, Amélie. *La Normandie romanesque et merveilleuse: traditions, légendes et superstitions populaires de cette province.* Paris and Rouen, 1845.

The chapter devoted to werewolves contains an analysis of *Bisclavret* (pp. 239-43).

101 Brereton, Georgine E. 'A Thirteenth-Century List of French Lays and Other Narrative Poems', *Modern Language Review,* XLV (1950), 40-5.

Shrewsbury School MS which mentions lays entitled *Bisclaueret, Frene, Laumual, Eliduc, Le cay cyuel* (probably *Chaitivel*), *Cheuerefoil, Milun, Yonech* and *Vygamer* (= *Guigemar?*).

102 Brightenback, Kristine. 'Remarks on the *Prologue* to Marie de France's *Lais'*, *Romance Philology,* XXX (1976-7), 168-77.

Marie's prologue provides clues to her view of her poetic craft and illustrates the way in which the *Lais* participate in the contemporary vernacular tradition. The expression *gloser la lettre* is both a homage to the classical *auctores* and a reflection of a common 12th- and 13th-century method of composition. In this article *Guigemar* is taken as an example of Marie's notion of gloss, a notion which helps us to understand the coherence of the whole collection and to see that in some *lais* Marie glosses herself.

103 Bromwich, Rachel. 'Celtic Dynastic Themes and the Breton Lays', *Etudes Celtiques,* IX (1960-1), 439-74.

An examination of two themes, the Transformed Hag and the Chase of the White Stag, both possessing dynastic significance in early Irish mythology. The white hind episode in *Guigemar* is discussed. *Lanval,* however, lacks the motif of the pursuit of the white hart found in *Graelent,* a lay which appears to preserve a more primitive version of the tale than Marie's text. The conclusion is drawn that 'Marie tended to substitute literary models for older popular elements in her sources'. A detailed and useful study.

104 —, ' A Note on the Breton Lays', *Medium Aevum,* XXVI (1957), 36-8.

Marie knew that narrative poems similar to her own existed in Breton. Older Breton prose-verse sagas had been recast in the form of narrative lays probably by the beginning of the twelfth century. There is thus no need to distinguish between the *contes* and the *lais* to which Marie refers (e.g., *Guigemar,* 19-21; *Eliduc,* 1181-4).

105 Brown, Jack D. 'Old French *estre* : a New Meaning', *Romance Notes,* XIV (1972-3), 597-8.

> *Guigemar,* MS S, 1. 226, contains an example of *estre* 'to go out': 'Nus n'i pot estre ne entrer' (MS H *eissir*). *Estre* with this meaning should thus be included in dictionaries of Old French.

106 Bruce, James D. *The Evolution of Arthurian Romance from the Beginnings down to the Year 1300.* 2 vols, 1923. 2nd ed., with supplement by Alfons Hilka, Baltimore: The Johns Hopkins Press, 1928. Reprint Gloucester, Mass.: Peter Smith, 1958.

> Contains summaries of the *Lais,* analyses and abundant bibliographical information (vol. I, pp. 52-66, vol. II, pp. 175-87, 387-8, 449-50).

107 Brugger, Ernst. 'Über die Bedeutung von *Bretagne, breton* in mittelalterlichen Texten', *Zeitschrift für französische Sprache und Literatur,* XX (1898), 79-162.

> Extensive material on Marie's place names (pp. 121-62). See items 108, 307 and 481.

108 —, 'Eigennamen in den *Lais* der Marie de France', *Zeitschrift für französische Sprache und Literatur,* LXIX (1927), 201-52, 381-484.

> An important article of immense erudition. Contains abundant documentation and an index to names discussed. See items 107, 307 and 491.

109 —, 'Die *Lais* der Marie de France', *Zeitschrift für französische Sprache und Literatur,* XLIX (1927), 116-55.

> A review of Warnke, *Die Lais der Marie de France,* 3rd ed. (item 17).

110 Bullock-Davies, Constance. 'The Form of the Breton Lay', *Medium Aevum,* XLII (1973), 18-31.

> A subtle analysis of the Breton/Briton manner of performing lays. It was not content but technical form that characterized the Breton lay. The title of the *lai* was carried by the harp-melody and to perform *in britunischer wise* (Gottfried von Strassburg, *Tristan*) and *si cum cil Bretun d'itiel fait costumier (Romance of Horn)* involved some kind of voice/harp technique with the voice providing a form of counterpoint to the harp melody, akin to the old Welsh art of *penillion*-singing. The origins of the Breton lay were also unusual. As Marie stresses, every Breton lay was composed of an *aventure* and a commemorative melody. By the time Marie began her collection, the Breton lay, belonging originally to a small, integrated society, had, as a performance, gone out of fashion.

111 —, 'Lanval and Avalon', *The Bulletin of the Board of Celtic Studies,* XXIII (1969), 128-42.

An important study of the origins of the story of Lanval with convincing arguments in favour of a North British provenance. The tale preserves the name of a Celtic god Lanovalus, worshipped, like Lug, by the banks of a swiftly flowing river near a tidal estuary. The reference to Carlisle (*Kardoel*, 1. 5) is not an invention of Marie's. The hero lived and loved in Carlisle and its neighbourhood and it is here too, in modern Burgh-by-Sands (Roman *Avalana* or *Aballava*) that his Avalon is probably located. His mistress, unmistakably a water-divinity, must be Morgen, 'Murigena', the 'sea-born', later Morgan la fée.

112 —, 'The Love-Messenger in *Milun*', *Nottingham Mediaeval Studies,* XVI (1972), 20-7.

A convincing demonstration that the *aventure* in *Milun* is localized in Gwent, in the area surrounding Caerleon and Caerwent. The 'dreit chemin' in 1. 177 would be the old Roman road running from Chepstow to Newport, the Julia Strata, which also occurs in *Yonec*, 1. 478. To the south and south-west of Caerleon there is still a natural breeding place for swans. Everything connected with the swan in *Milun* can be accounted for in terms of the reality of its day. Summary in *Bibliographical Bulletin of the International Arthurian Society*, XXI (1969), 148.

Review by:

.1 F. Masai, *Scriptorium*, XXVIII (1974), 355.

113 —, ' Marie, Abbess of Shaftesbury, and her Brothers', *The English Historical Review,* LXXX (1965), 314-22.

Concerns the three brothers of the Abbess of Shaftesbury, William, Durand and Gilbert, all influential officers at the royal court who came to England from the present-day St Mars d'Outillé near Le Mans. If the abbess was Marie de France, the latter's mother was thus the Lady of Outillé. See items 183, 184 and 232.

114 —, *'L'uevre Salemun', Medium Aevum,* XXIX (1960), 173-83.

Concerns the interpretation of *Guigemar*, 1. 172. The expression *l'uevre Salemun* was a topical phrase which may possibly be explained by reference to Henry of Blois and his 'sharp practices over other people's Byzantine antiques and genuine *opera Salomonis'*. See items 72, 81, 284 and 466.

115 Burger, André. ' La Tradition manuscrite du lai de *Lanval'*, in *Linguistique et philologie romanes, Xe congrès international de linguistique et de philologie romanes, Actes,* publiés par G.

Straka, 3 vols, Paris: Klincksieck (Actes et Colloques, IV), 1965, vol. II, pp. 655-66.

The four MSS containing *Lanval* (HPCS) have been variously classified: e.g. HP-CS (Hoepffner, item 228; Segre, item 413), HP-CS (Rychner, item 14). Burger proposes convincingly H-CPS, as in several passages CPS are united against H. It is more difficult to establish a subdivision in the group CPS, but the most significant common faults link P and S.

116   Burgess, Glyn S. *'Orgueil* and *Fierté* in Twelfth-century French', *Zeitschrift für romanische Philologie,* LXXXIX (1973), 103-22.

Contains observations on the use in the *Lais* of *fier* and *orgueilleux* (pp. 119-21).

117   Cagnon, Maurice. *'Chievrefueil* and the Ogamic Tradition', *Romania,* XCI (1970), 238-55.

Tristan's message to Iseut may have been carved in ogamic script. The length of the message and the difficulty of reading it from horseback would thus no longer constitute a problem. Lines 60-1 ('De sun ami bien conustra/Le bastun quant el le verra') would refer to Iseut's recognition of Tristan's individual style of carving and l. 82 ('Tutes les lettres i conut') would also take on added significance.

118   *Capone, S. *Eliduc: Storia d'amore medievale.* Naples, 1939.
Offers a rhymed version of *Eliduc.*

119   Cargo, Robert T. 'Marie de France's *Le Laustic* and Ovid's *Metamorphoses', Comparative Literature,* XVIII (1966), 162-6.

A suggestion that the lady in *Laüstic* sends her lover an embroidered message (*escrire* in l. 136 will mean "to show, to depict"), thus recalling the method of communication used by Philomela in Book VI of the *Metamorphoses.*

120   Chabaille, P. 'Marie de France', in *Nouvelle Biographie générale, depuis les temps les plus reculés jusqu'à nos jours.* 46 vols, Paris: Firmin Didot Frères, 1857-66, vol. XXXIII (1860), cols 732-7.

Marie was born in Compiègne and flourished in the thirteenth century. Her fifteen *lais* were probably dedicated to Henry III. Accepts Legrand d'Aussy's identification (item 56) of *le cunte Willame* as Guillaume de Dampierre (died 1251).

121   Chefneux, Hélène. 'Les Fables dans la Tapisserie de Bayeux', *Romania,* LX (1934), 1-35, 153-94.

The nine fables in the Bayeux tapestry are found in their entirety only in Marie's *Fables* and the London-Brussels-Göttingen (LBG) collection. The source of the Bayeux fables was probably a collection analogous to that used by Marie and the compiler of the LBG collection. Concludes, after a useful summary of earlier theories of the relationship between Marie and her source, that the English collection by Alfred did exist. An English source for the Bayeux tapestry is thus possible.

122 Chotzen, Th. M. *'Bisclavret'*, *Etudes Celtiques*, II (1937), 33-44.

The term *bisclavret* derives from *Bleidd llafar*, 'le cher petit loup parlant, le bon loup fatidique'. The name is thus inappropriate for Marie's were-wolf, but she may not have concerned herself with or even understood its real meaning.

123 Cigada, Sergio. *La leggenda medievale del Cervo Biancho e le origini della 'matière de Bretagne'*. Rome: Accademia Nazionale dei Lincei, 1965 (Atti della Accademia Nazionale dei Lincei, 1965, Memorie: Classe di Scienze Morali, Storiche e Filologiche, serie VIII, volume XI, fascicolo I), 1965.

The role of the white stag in several Old French *lais* is discussed on pp. 22-9 with remarks on *Guigemar* and its relationship to *Graelent* (pp. 22-4).

124 Clédat, Léon. 'Les *Lais* de Marie de France', in *Histoire de la langue et de la littérature française des origines à 1900*, ed. L. Petit de Julleville. 8 vols, Paris: Colin, 1896-99, vol. I, pp. 285-302.

An analysis of *Lanval, Deus Amanz, Yonec, Laüstic, Chevrefoil* and *Eliduc*.

125 —, 'Oeuvres narratives du moyen âge: analyses et extraits traduits', *Revue de Philologie Française et Provençale* (ancienne *Revue des Patois)*, VIII (1894), 161-264.

Marie's *Lais* are discussed on pp. 161-205.

126 Cocito, Luciana. *Saggi di filologia romanza*. Genoa: Bozzi, 1971.

Contains a chapter entitled 'Per un *lai* di Maria di Francia (*Chevrefoil*)', pp. 57-67. Summarizes some earlier interpretations of *Chevrefoil* and concludes that the message was not written in full or in part on the branch and that Spitzer's view (item 424) is correct. However, the words explaining the meaning of the symbol are Tristan's, not Iseut's. For Tristan it is the bough which must express the indissoluble nature of his love.

127   Cohen, Gustave. 'Marie de France, le lai des *Deux Amants'*, *Mercure de France*, CCLXV (1936), 61-8.
A transposition of the *Deus Amanz* into modern French is preceded by remarks on the survival of the legend of the Two Lovers in local tradition. See items 44 and 128.

128   — , *La Vie littéraire en France au moyen-âge*. Paris: Tallandier, 1949.
Contains a section entitled 'Notre première femme de lettres : Marie de France' (pp. 113-17). Readable, but superficial.

129   Conigliani, Camilla, 'L'amore e l'avventura nei *Lais* di Maria di Francia', *Archivum Romanicum*, II (1918), 281-95.
The *Lais*, in which love and adventure are (as in all narrative literature) the essential elements, were composed at a time when contact with Celtic peoples and the imitation of Provençal poets were modifying the chivalric ideal. Marie's particular conception of love is simply that it is the dominating force in life. Her notion of adventure is more natural and more primitive than that of Chrétien de Troyes.

130   Constans, L. *Marie de Compiègne d'après l'Evangile aux femmes: texte publié pour la première fois dans son intégrité d'après les quatre manuscrits connus*. Paris: Franck, 1876.
Accepts Marie de France as author of the *Evangile aux femmes*. Contains a general section on the *Lais* (pp. 9-12; dedicated to Henry III around 1245) and the *Fables* (pp. 13-20; dedicated to Guillaume de Dampierre about 1248). See item 319.

131   Contini, Gianfranco. 'Su Marie de France', in *Esercizî di lettura*. Florence: Felici Le Monnier, 1947, pp. 277-84.
General remarks. Superficial.

132   Coppin, Joseph. *Amour et mariage dans la littérature française du nord au moyen-âge*. Paris: Librairie d'Argences, 1961.
General remarks on Marie, pp. 68-70.

133   Cottrell, Robert D. *'Le Lai du Laustic*: From Physicality to Spirituality,' *Philological Quarterly*, XLVII (1968), 499-505.
An examination of the nightingale and its 'symbolic content'. The nightingale is 'the central character in the *lai*' (500) and through it the lovers exteriorize their love. In committing the dead bird to a small shrine the knight spiritualizes the love which then 'no longer exists in the realm of temporality and physicality' (504). This spiritualization of love is modelled on the theological doctrine of transubstantiation.

134   Cowling, Samuel T. 'The Image of the Tournament in Marie

de France's *Le Chaitivel'*, *Romance Notes,* XVI (1974-5), 686-91.

Marie relies on images to convey feelings and the central image of *Chaitivel* is the tournament. The knights who perform and the lady who watches actualize in the tournament the ideal code of chivalric existence. The splendour of the code contrasts, however, with the suffering of those submitted to it. In this lay the lady also suffers, and she will know no further romance. She is not to be seen as an example of selfishness.

135 Crosland, Jessie. *Medieval French Literature.* Oxford: Blackwell, 1956.

Contains a substantial section on the *Lais,* pp. 92-102.

136 Cross, Tom P. 'The Celtic Elements in the Lays of *Lanval* and *Graelent'*, *Modern Philology*, XII (1914-15), 585-644.

Contains sections on the fairy mistress in the world of mortals, the fountain scene, the character of the fairy mistress, the *ges* or injunction to silence, fairy gifts, the loss of the fairy mistress, the return of the fairy mistress. The abundant and useful documentation is seen as justifying the claims of the authors of *Graelent* and *Lanval* that their lays are based on traditions current amongst the Celts.

137 —, 'The Celtic *Fée* in *Launfal'*, in *Anniversary Papers by Colleagues and Pupils of George Lyman Kittredge.* Boston and London: Ginn and Company, 1913, pp. 377-87.

Concerns principally *Sir Launfal,* but offers a number of comments on *Lanval.*

138 —, ' The Celtic Origin of the Lay of *Yonec'*, *Revue Celtique,* XXXI (1910), 413-71. Also in separate print, Paris: Champion, 1911 and in shortened form in *Studies in Philology,* XI (1913), 26-60.

Although several features of *Yonec* are encountered in Classical or Oriental tradition or elsewhere, the lay represents a combination of three Celtic motifs: 1) A supernatural lover visits a mortal in the form of a bird, enters into a union with her and is discovered by the husband, who slays or wounds him; 2) A fairy lover makes a woman his mistress and departs predicting the birth of a famous son, who is later recognized by his father by means of a ring or token; 3) A woman is carried off to the Other World by her fairy lover. These motifs were combined under the influence of the Inclusa theme. See items 241, 253 and 344.

139 Damon, S. Foster. 'Marie de France: Psychologist of Courtly Love', *Publications of the Modern Language Association of*

America, XLIV (1929), 968-96.

The *lais* are seen as realistic (subdivided thematically into pairs, *Laüstic-Chevrefoil, Eliduc-Chaitivel, Deus Amanz-Equitan, Milun-Le Fresne)* and supernatural *(Bisclavret, Guigemar, Guingamor, Lanval, Yonec)*. The latter are analyzed perceptively as symbolic character studies or studies of introverts through symbolic supernaturalism. Symbolism is considered, perhaps unwisely, as incidental in the realistic lays and all-pervasive in the supernatural lays. The chief protagonists of the supernatural lays are viewed in psychological terms, Guigemar as a perverse sensualist, his beloved as a suppressed puritan, and the doe, activator of the *aventure*, as innocence betrayed. The lady in *Yonec* is a suppressed non-puritan, her lover an imaginary ideal destroyed. The real father of Yonec is the sensual old husband, idealized by a lonely woman. An important and influential article.

140   Dargan, E.P. 'Cock and Fox: A Critical Study of the History and Sources of the Mediaeval Fable', *Modern Philology*, IV (1906-7), 38-65.
       Concerns Marie's fable *De vulpe et gallo* (ed. Warnke, no. LX), which is compared in detail with other extant versions of the same tale. Marie's version probably derives in part from Phaedrus and in part from a folk-tale about the wolf.

141   Daunou, P.C.F. 'Discours sur l'état des lettres (treizième siècle)', in *Histoire de la France*, XVI (1824), pp. 1-254.
       Marie is discussed on pp. 171, 209-13, 223-4.

142   Davison, Muriel. 'Marie de France's *Lai de Lanval*, 31-38', *The Explicator*, XXI, 2 (Oct. 1962), item 12.
       A short note offering a structural explanation for Marie's comment on the unhappiness of a foreigner who has no one to whom to turn for support. This is not an autobiographical *cri de coeur*, but an attempt by Marie to cover up and account for the deliberate disfavour and 'mean treatment' of which Lanval is the object.

143   De Caluwé, Jacques. La Conception de l'amour dans le lai d'*Eliduc* de Marie de France', *Le Moyen Age*, LXXVII (1971), 53-77.
       The text of *Eliduc* is divided into six sections: prologue (ll. 1-28), Eliduc's departure and his exploits at Totnes (ll. 29-264), the birth of love (ll. 265-549), the conflict (ll. 550-952), Guildeluëc's sacrifice (ll. 953-1144), epilogue (ll. 1145-84). Marie's source is seen, probably correctly, as a tale of some substance containing all the principal elements found in *Eliduc,* not as a *chanson* (Rychner). Marie reduced the military exploits in order to concentrate on the problem of love.

The conception of love is compared to Agnès Varda's film *Le Bonheur.*

144   De Feo, Anna S. 'Alcuni *lais* di Marie de France ', *Rivista d'Italia,* XI (1908), 202-27.
General remarks on the *Lais* and an analysis of the *Deus Amanz* (pp. 207-11), *Yonec* (pp. 211-14), *Laüstic* (pp. 214-15) and *Eliduc* (pp. 215-26).

145   Dehousse, Françoise. *Sainte-Beuve: ancienne littérature (partie médiévale), cours professé à l'Université de Liège, 1848-9.* Paris: Les Belles Lettres (Bibliothèque de la Faculté de Philosophie et Lettres de l'Université de Liège, CLXXXVII), 1971.
Marie de France is the subject of pp. 543-52.

146   Delbouille, Maurice. *'Ceo fu la summe de l'escrit... (Chievrefoil,* 61 ss.)', in *Mélanges de langue et de littérature du moyen âge et de la Renaissance offerts à Jean Frappier par ses collègues, ses élèves et ses amis.* Geneva: Droz, 1970, vol. I, pp. 207-16.
An excellent summary of earlier interpretations of ll. 61-78 of *Chevrefoil* is followed by a suggestion concerning the *escrit* sent by Tristan to Iseut and mentioned in ll. 61 and 109. The letter in question may have been sent on a previous occasion (cf. ll. 57-8). Iseut would be on the watch for any hazel branch she might see on the ground. All the elements in this *lai,* both narrative and psychological, are seen as dependent on the lost French *Tristan* text composed about 1165 and not on a *lai* of *Chevrefoil* making no mention of the two lovers. See item 330.

147   —, *'El chief de cest comencement...* (Marie de France, Prologue de *Guigemar)',* in *Etudes de civilisation médiévale (IXe-XIIe siècles). Mélanges offerts à Edmond-René Labande.* Poitiers: Centre d'Etudes Supérieures de Civilisation Médiévale, 1974, pp. 185-96.
The general prologue to the *Lais* and the prologue to *Guigemar* do not present any of the difficulties which certain scholars have seen in them. Critics have been right to attribute the twelve *lais* of MS H to Marie. If one interprets *comencement* in l. 56 of the general prologue as 'prologue' and the expression *el chief de cest comencement* as 'at the end of this prologue', there is no need to follow Baum (item 85, pp. 37ff), who contests the authenticity of the prologue to *Guigemar* and consequently that of Marie's signature in l. 3. See item 416.

148   —, ' Le Nom et le personnage d'Equitan', *Le Moyen Age,*
       LXIX (1963), 315-23.

An interesting discussion of the interpretation of the form *Nauns*
(*nains,* S) in l. 12 of *Equitan.* Rejecting the identification of *Nauns* as a
noun formed from *Namnetes* (Warnke, Hoepffner and others) and
Brugger's emendation to *Vanes* (item 107, p. 143 and item 108,
pp. 240-1), Delbouille proposes to see Equitan as 'sire des nains' (cf.
Chrétien de Troyes, *Erec et Enide,* ed. Roques, ll. 1941-2: 'Li sires des
nains vint aprés,/Bilis, li rois d'Antipodés'). Béroul's dwarf Frocin(e) was
probably called Aquitan in the primitive *Tristan.* Gottfried speaks of
Melot petit von Aquitân and Eilhart of *Aquitain der arge* (the form
Aquitan occurs twice in MS S of *Equitan,* ll. 11 and 313). The *lai* would
thus reflect not a human legend situated in the region of Nantes but
Celtic stories of giants and dwarves. The name Equitan, suggests
Delbouille, derives from a Latin text in which a dwarf rides a mount
well suited to his size: e.g., *nanus (caprum) equitans.*

149   Del Monte, Alberto and Anna M. Raugei. *Introduzione alla*
       lettura dei Lais di Maria di Francia. Appunti dalle lezione del
       Prof. Alberto Del Monte a cura della Dott. Anna Maria
       Raugei. Milan: Cisalpino-Goliardica (Università degli Studi
       di Milano, Facoltà di Lettere e Filosofia, Cattedra di Filologia
       Romanza, anno accademico 1972-3), 1973, 121 pp.

Chapter headings are: (1) Maria di Francia e le sue opere; (2) Cronologia
delle opere di Maria; (3) Problema del testo; (4) Successo e originalità
dei *Lais;* (5) Origini della materia di Bretagna; (6) Natura dei *lais*
celtici; (7) Il *lai* come genere letterario; (8) La letteratura popolare e i
Lais di Maria di Francia; (9) Motivi e antecedenti dei *Lais* di Maria di
Francia; (10) I *Lais* come opera letteraria.

149a   Di Stefano, Giuseppe. 'Marie de France', in *Dizionario*
       critico della letteratura francese, diretto da Franco Simone.
       2 vols, Turin: Unione Tipografico-Editrice Torinese, 1971,
       vol. II, pp. 741-5.

Thorough general introduction to Marie's works.

150   Dinaux, Arthur. *Les Trouvères de la Flandre et du Tournaisis.*
       Paris, 1839. Reprint, Geneva: Slatkine, 1969.

Contains a section on Marie de France (pp. 309-16). Marie was born in
Compiègne at the beginning of the thirteenth century, and attracted to
Flanders by the protection of Guillaume de Dampierre. *Graelent* and
the *Lai de l'Epine* are attributed to Marie in addition to the Harley
collection.

151   Donovan, Mortimer J. *The Breton Lay: A Guide to Varieties.*

Notre Dame, Indiana: Univ. of Notre Dame Press, 1969.
A well-documented and wide-ranging study. Chapter I is entitled 'Marie de France and the Breton Lay' (pp. 1-64).

152 — , 'Priscian and the Obscurity of the Ancients', *Speculum*, XXXVI (1961), 75-80.
A discussion of ll. 9-16 of the Prologue. These lines are ambiguous, but Marie seems to have regarded the ancients as writing obscurely because they lived too early to see the full development of their meaning. But they were not deliberately obscure. Lines 15-16 ('K'i peüssent gloser la lettre,/E de lur sen le surplus mettre') refers to the clearing up of obscurities or correcting and reworking one's sources. Marie has changed the meaning of Priscian's comments in the opening sentence of the *Institutiones*, as do other twelfth-century writers (Bishop Otto of Freising, Andrew of St Victor, Henricus Brito, etc.).

153 Dragonetti, Roger. 'Le Lai narratif de Marie de France'. See item 518 (Addenda, p. 112).

154 Dubuis, Roger. *Les Cent Nouvelles nouvelles et la tradition de la nouvelle en France au moyen âge.* Grenoble: Presses Universitaires, 1973.
Contains a substantial section devoted to *lais,* with abundant references to those of Marie (pp. 307-479). Deals with a wide range of structural and thematic points, including a study of love in the *lais* (pp. 376-90) and the element of *merveilleux* (pp. 363-75).

155 Du Chesne, André. *Les Oeuvres de Maistre Alain Chartier.* Paris, 1617.
Speaks of a 'traducteur des Fables d'Esope en vieil François' (p. 861), but does not name Marie.

156 Dunn, Charles W. *The Foundling and the Werwolf: a Literary Historical study of Guillaume de Palerne.* Toronto: Univ. (Department of English, Studies and Texts, VIII), 1960.
Deals at some length with the werewolf and related themes in medieval romance, and cites Marie a number of times when discussing points of detail.

157 Durand-Monti, Paul. 'Encore le bâton de *Chevrefoil'*, *Bibliographical Bulletin of the International Arthurian Society,* XII (1960), 117-18.
Lines 51-4 of *Chevrefoil* can be explained by a Norman custom.

158   Durdan, A.-L. *Le Lai des Deux-Amants, légende neustrienne de Marie de France: commentaire et adaptation.* Mâcon: Protat Frères, 1907.
The king in the *Deus Amanz* is identified as Charles the Bald, who lived in Pitres from A.D. 861 to 869. The daughter referred to in the text must have been illegitimate. The young man would be the son of the count of Hasdans. Text of the *lai* on pp. 27-33, verse translation pp. 35-41. A few useful comments, but little of significance. Salerne is identified as the 'pays de Salerne' (Eure) near Brionne, in the diocese of Lisieux.

159   Duval, A. 'Poésies de Marie de France', in *Histoire littéraire de la France,* XIX (1838), pp. 791-809.
General discussion, including an analysis of the *Espurgatoire* (pp. 799-804). The *Lais* were probably dedicated to Henry III, the *Fables* to William Longsword. See also pp. 716-20 for a study of *Lanval.*

160   Du Verdier, Antoine. *La Bibliothèque d'Antoine Du Verdier, seigneur de Vauprivas, contenant le catalogue de tous ceux qui ont escrit ou traduict en françois et autres dialectes de ce royaume.* Lyon, 1585.
Speaks of the *Fables* of Marie de France (pp. 848-9) in terms almost identical to those of Fauchet (item 165). See item 276.

161   Eberwein, Elena. 'Die *Aventure* in den altfranzösischen *Lais*', in *Zur Deutung mittelalterlicher Existenz.* Bonn and Cologne (Kölner romanistische Arbeiten, VII), 1933, pp. 27-53.
An important and densely written study of the concept of *aventure.* Offers in particular an extended analysis of *Laüstic, Bisclavret* and *Lanval.*

162   Faral, Edmond, *Le Manuscrit 19152 du fonds français de la Bibliothèque Nationale: reproduction phototypique publiée avec une introduction.* Paris: Droz, 1934.
The MS reproduced here contains Marie's *Fables,* fols 15a-24d.

163   — , 'Marie de France: *Les Lais*', in *Histoire de la littérature française illustrée,* ed. Joseph Bédier and Paul Hazard. Paris: Larousse, 1923, new ed. 1948, vol. I, pp. 23-4 (new ed., pp. 32-3).
Brief but interesting remarks. Marie wrote around 1175 at the earliest. She came after Chrétien de Troyes. The *nobles reis* is probably *Henri au Cort Mantel,* count William probably William Marshal.

164   Fasciano, Domenico. 'La Mythologie du lai *Les Deux Amants',*
      Rivista di Cultura Classica e Medioevale, XVI (1974), 79-85.
      The *Deus Amanz* recalls in its origin, structure and symbolism a number
      of classical legends (e.g., those of Pyramus and Thisbe and Icarus). The
      ascent of the mountain is both a courtly test and an initiation rite, the
      passage from the profane to the sacred, a means of transcending the
      human condition and penetrating to a higher cosmic world. In its
      symbolism the philtre is analogous to classical remedies for overcoming
      human powerlessness and is linked to man's struggle against degener-
      ation. Initially the vial is a phallic symbol as it contains the young man's
      sexual potency and the two lovers, in the grip of an Electra and an
      Oedipus complex, ascend the mountain in accordance with a sexual
      rhythm. When the vial is broken, an act which liberates the girl from
      her complex, its contents make the ground fertile, a fact which re-
      inforces the link between this text and regeneration myths.

165   Fauchet, Claude. *Recueil de l'origine de la langue et poesie*
      françoise: ryme et romans, plus les noms et sommaire des
      oeuvres de CXXVII poetes François, vivans avant l'an
      M.CCC. Paris, 1581. Reprint, Geneva: Slatkine, 1972.
      Book II, item LXXXIIII, is entitled 'Marie de France', the first attested
      example of this appellation. The entry reads: 'Marie de France, ne porte
      ce surnom pour ce qu'elle fust du sang des Rois: mais pource qu'elle
      estoit natifve de France, car elle dit,

         Au finement de cet escrit,
         Me nommerai par remembrance,
         Marie ai nom, si sui de France.

      Elle a mis en vers François les fables d'Esope moralisees, qu'elle dit
      avoir translatees d'Anglois en François. Pour l'amour au Conte
      Guilleaume,

         Le plus vaillant de ce Roiaume.'
      Cf. Baum, item 85, pp. 61-2.

166   Ferguson, Mary H. 'Folklore in the *Lais* of Marie de France',
      The Romanic Review, LVII (1966), 3-24.
      Constitutes a useful introduction to a fruitful line of enquiry. Folklore
      motifs are listed in accordance with the classification of Stith Thompson.
      The author suggests that the narrative direction adopted by Marie is
      consistently opposed to that of the folktales.

167   Ferrante, Joan M. *Woman as Image in Medieval Literature,*
      from the Twelfth Century to Dante. New York and London:
      Columbia University Press, 1975.
      Love in the *Lais* is seen as a facet of female as well as male psychology.

Love is not merely an inspiration. It is a means of overcoming the pains of this world and the bonds of society, for love exists in the mind, which is free to act as it wishes. Through love the individual can find his will and thus escape domination by hostile forces (pp. 95-7).

168   Feugère, Fernand. 'La Volière de Marie de France', *Défense de la Langue Française,* LIV (1970), 9-11.

About sixty Modern French words occur for the first time in Marie's writings. Particularly noteworthy are words from the domain of nature (*rossignol, moineau, pinson, mésange, coucou, chèvrefeuille, sanglier*, etc.) and 'feminine' words (*broder, boucle, cheville, gril, rôtir, éplucher*, etc.).

169   Finoli, Anna Maria. 'La volpe e il corvo nei rifacimenti medievali di Fedro, in Maria di Francia e nel *Roman de Renart* di Pierre de Saint-Cloud', *Annali della Facoltà di Lettere e Filosofia dell'Università degli Studi di Milano,* XXIII (1970), 317-28. Also in separate print, Varese and Milan: Nicola, 1970, 12pp.

Includes useful remarks on the source of Marie's fable *De corvo et vulpe* (ed. Warnke, no. XIII).

170   Fitz, Brewster E. 'The Prologue to the *Lais* of Marie de France and the Parable of the Talents: Gloss and Monetary Metaphor', *Modern Language Notes,* XC (1975), 558-64.

The Parable of the Talents, to which Marie refers in ll. 1-8 of the Prologue, is seen as providing a 'semantic and thematic key' to the entire Prologue. The monetary metaphor contained in the Parable is the 'unifying metaphor of textual production that governs Marie's exegetic undertaking'.

171   — , 'The Storm Episode and the Weasel Episode: Sacrificial Casuistry in Marie de France's *Eliduc'*, *Modern Language Notes,* LXXXIX (1974), 542-9.

The sailor's interpretation of the storm (ll. 830-40) is accurate in that a communal act of violence is required to abate the violence of the storm and to bring the boat safely to shore. But by breaking his oath of silence (ll. 777-8) the sailor becomes the only clearly guilty passenger and causes Guilliadun's apparent death. He is thus a perfect scapegoat for the sacrifice. However, Guilliadun as a result of her involvement in an intended adultery is also a sacrificial victim and she lives again only when another victim is substituted for her. This occurs in the weasel episode in which the weasel, appearing from beneath the altar, is killed violently for imparting impurity to the sleeping girl. Guildeluec restores order by an act of charity and self-sacrifice.

172 Flum, P.N. 'Additional Thoughts on Marie de France',
Romance Notes, III (1961-2), 53-6.
Supports Holmes' identification of Marie as the wife of Hugh Talbot
and the daughter of Galeran II, count of Meulan(see items 173 & 234).
Flum cites two additional sources which speak of Galeran and his wife
Agnes, and provides confirmation of Hugh Talbot's title as baron of
Cleuville.

173 —, 'Marie de France and the Talbot Family Connections',
Romance Notes, VII (1965-6), 83-6.
Concerns the relationship of Walter of Claville and Hugh Talbot (see
items 172 and 234). The Red Book of the Exchequer and certain
documentary collections contain entries suggesting a link between the
two families. Fairbairn's *Crests of the Leading Families of Great Britain
and Ireland* shows a Colwell family of England with the talbot hound on
its crest and a Colvil family of Scotland whose crest displays the talbot
hound's head.

174 Flutre, Louis-Fernand. *Table des noms propres avec toutes
leurs variantes figurant dans les romans du moyen âge écrits
en français ou en provençal et actuellement publiés ou
analysés.* Poitiers: Centre d'Etudes Supérieures de Civilisation
Médiévale, 1962.
Includes geographical, ethnic and personal names from the *Lais.*

175 Foulet, Lucien. 'English Words in the *Lais* of Marie de
France', *Modern Language Notes,* XX (1905), 109-11.
The two English terms in the *Lais (nihtegale, Laüstic,* 6; *gotelef,
Chevrefoil,* 115) do not indicate that Marie was translating from an
English source. They were probably inspired by the *Brut* of Wace (esp.
ll. 7473 ff. and 8383ff.).

176 —, 'Marie de France et les lais bretons', *Zeitschrift für
romanische Philologie,* XXIX (1905), 19-56, 293-322.
Wide-ranging discussion. Part I attempts to demonstrate, not always
with convincing results, that all the anonymous *lais* were composed
after those of Marie, and that almost all make use of her texts, even to
the point of plagiarism. Part II begins with an analysis of the prologue
to *Guigemar* and the Prologue to the whole collection. The prologue to
Guigemar, the first *lai* composed by Marie, introduces the collection; the
general prologue is in fact an epilogue. There follows a useful study of
the terms *lai* and *conte* in the *Lais,* of the link between French narrative
and lyrical *lais* and that between Marie's *Lais* and the Breton *lais*
to which she refers. Foulet concludes that 'les lais de Marie de France

sont des contes qui étaient déjà des contes — et probablement l'avaient toujours été — dans la tradition à laquelle elle les empruntait' (p. 315) and that 'l'histoire des lais français commence et s'arrête à Marie' (p. 319).
Review by:

.1   J. Bédier, *Romania*, XXXIV (1905), 479-80 and XXXV (1906), 137.
Bédier thinks that the *Lai de l'Espine* was written by Marie.

177   —, 'Marie de France et la légende du Purgatoire de Saint Patrice', *Romanische Forschungen*, XXII (1908), 599-627.
An important and erudite study. From an analysis of the twenty-three surviving MSS of the *Tractatus* of Henry of Saltrey it is possible to establish what belongs to Henry's original text and what to later scribes and redactors, who made substantial interpolations and additions. But Marie knew the *Tractatus* when it had reached the close of its evolution. A study of the proper names in the *Tractatus* suggests a date of composition not earlier than 1170, more likely after 1180 or even 1185. For the *Espurgatoire* it is impossible to fix a *terminus ad quem*, but it may well have been composed shortly after 1185. Marie saw in the account by Henry not an edifying or theological narrative, but simply an interesting story, which she tells with the sincerity and absence of humour which are characteristic of the *Lais*.

178   —, 'Marie de France et la légende de Tristan', *Zeitschrift für romanische Philologie*, XXXII (1908), 161-83, 257-89.
A dense and detailed study embracing a wide range of topics relating to the *Lais*. In the second third of the 12th century the term *lai* designated simply an 'air de musique que les Bretons du temps d'Arthur exécutaient sur la harpe'. Marie had the idea of composing *contes* to explain the link between these tunes and a variety of *aventures*. Her efforts gave rise to a 200-year tradition in which lays multiplied, particularly in the *romans d'aventure*. *Lanval* is the first Arthurian romance and without Marie an important aspect of Tristan's poetic personality would have remained unknown. Marie knew the earliest French Tristan text, but not the *Tristan* of Thomas. It was Marie who inspired Thomas. Behind the *lais* of *Guigemar* and *Lanval*, and the *Tristan* of Thomas, we catch a glimpse of a confused group of French works which must have charmed the contemporaries of Henry I and Stephen, but which were not sufficiently elegant for the court of Henry II.

179   —, 'Le Prologue du *Franklin's Tale* et les lais bretons', *Zeitschrift für romanische Philologie*, XXX (1906), 698-711.
Concerns principally the meaning of the term 'lay' in Middle English and the influence of Marie on Chaucer. Concludes that: 'L'histoire du lai narratif — le mot et le genre — est la même en Angleterre qu'en France'.

180 —, *Le Roman de Renard.* Paris: Champion (Bibliothèque de l'Ecole des Hautes Etudes: Sciences historiques et philologiques, CCXI), 1914.

Contains numerous references to the *Fables,* esp. pp. 132-64, pp. 564-51.

181 —, 'Thomas and Marie in their Relation to the *Conteurs',* *Modern Language Notes,* XXIII (1908), 205-8.

On the interpretation of the *Tristan* of Thomas, ll. 2116-18 ('Oï en ai de plusur gent, /Asez sai que chescun en dit', ed. Bédier) and *Chevrefoil,* ll. 5-7 ('Plusurs le me unt cunté e dit/E jeo l'ai trové en escrit'). Examples of *dire* and *escrire* in Marie are quoted, terms which Marie does not always keep distinct.

182 Foulon, Charles. 'Marie de France et la Bretagne', *Annales de Bretagne,* LX (1952-3), 243-58.

Marie's knowledge of England and Normandy is more thorough than her knowledge of Brittany. But she does show an awareness of the social situation in Brittany, describing accurately knights who leave their country to seek a reputation elsewhere (e.g. *Guigemar,* 51; *Milun,* 121-2), young knights who spend their time at tournaments and spend all the money they earn (*Laüstic,* 21), knights who must think of contracting a rich marriage (e.g. *Le Fresne,* 329-31), etc. The life and habits of Breton women are also depicted, particularly in *Le Fresne* (e.g. 203-6, 413-17) and *Milun* (e.g. 96-104). Such descriptions would have pleased the Breton nobility surrounding Henry II which formed part of Marie's audience and readers. Foulon concludes that Marie knew at least some of her tales by means of an oral tradition stemming from bilingual (Breton or Welsh) storytellers.

183 Fox, John C. 'Marie de France', *English Historical Review,* XXV (1910), 303-6.

Marie is identified as Mary, abbess of Shaftesbury, natural daughter of Geoffrey Plantagenet, Count of Anjou, the father of Henry II. See items 113, 184 and 232.

Review by:
.1 E. Faral, *Romania,* XXXIX (1910), 625.

184 —, 'Mary, Abbess of Shaftesbury', *English Historical Review,* XXVI (1911), 317-26.

Evidence from charters in the Shaftesbury register shedding light on the life of the abbess Mary, but in no way confirming the identification with Marie de France. The earliest record of Mary as abbess is in a charter of 1181. See items 113, 183 and 232.

185 Francis, Elizabeth A. 'A Comment on *Chevrefoil',* in *Medieval*

Miscellany Presented to Eugène Vinaver. Manchester: Manchester University Press; New York: Barnes and Noble, 1965, pp. 136-45.

Lends support to the idea of an explanatory letter sent by Tristan to Iseut in advance of their meeting. Contains a useful, but not decisive, study of the terms *summe, escrit* and *mander* in an attempt to elucidate ll. 61-2. Parallels are suggested between *Chevrefoil* and *Milun*.

186   —, 'Marie de France et son temps', *Romania, LXXII* (1951), 78-99.

An important and closely argued study, in which the established facts concerning Marie and her work are placed in the contemporary geographical and historical context. The moral at the end of a fable provides useful information concerning the public to which the Fables were addressed. Their practical philosophy suggests a turbulent, ambitious and scheming society of barons and *chevaliers*, in which fortunes were made by personal dynamism and where fidelity and the choice of one's lord were of fundamental importance. A similar public would have appreciated the *Lais*, in which military honours, court favours and the king's *riches duns* replace the *gain* and *aveir* of the Fables. In general the *Lais* reflect the political rivalries of Henry II's kingdom in which administrative appointments often went to those who had supported his grandfather and whose families would have welcomed the dynastic references which several of the *Lais* seem to contain.

187   —, 'The Trial in *Lanval*', in *Studies in French Language and Mediæval Literature Presented to Professor Mildred K. Pope*. Manchester: Manchester University Press (Publications of the University of Manchester, CCLXVIII), 1939, pp. 115-24.

If Marie was copying in *Lanval* the trial of Daire le Roux in the *Roman de Thèbes* (see Hoepffner, item 216), she was also influenced by contemporary legal procedure. Her legal vocabulary corresponds very little to that of the *Thèbes*, but considerably to that of actual trials.

188   Frank, Grace, 'Marie de France and the Tristram Legend', *Publications of the Modern Language Association of America, LXIII* (1948), 405-11.

The whole of the message reported in *Chevrefoil*, ll. 65ff., was transcribed on the tablet. No prior communication had been sent to Iseut by Tristan. The scene in *Chevrefoil* embraces the past and foreshadows the future. It recalls in particular the episode in other versions in which Tristan fashions wood chips with a knife and throws them into a stream, as a signal to Iseut.

189   Frappier, Jean. *'D'amors, par amors'*, *Romania*, LXXXVIII (1967), 433-74.
The evidence from the *Lais* is discussed on pp. 442-3. *Eliduc* is the only lay in which the expression *amer par amur(s)* occurs (ll. 349 and 420).

190   —, 'Contribution au débat sur le lai du *Chèvrefeuille'*, in *Mélanges de linguistique et de littérature romanes à la mémoire d'István Frank.*. Sarrebruck: Universität des Saarlandes (Annales Universitatis Saraviensis, VI), 1957, pp. 215-24.
In opposition to scholars who consider that Tristan sent a message to Iseut warning her of his presence and explaining the symbolism of the hazel and the honeysuckle, Frappier follows Spitzer (item 424) and Hatcher (item 210) and sees Iseut's understanding of the situation as a spontaneous reaction. But this is not a miracle or pure intuition, as Spitzer and Hatcher maintain. Marie's reference to a previous episode of the same kind (ll. 57-8) prepares the way for the present incident and provides a rational explanation for Iseut's response to the hazel branch.
Reviews by:
.1   S. Cigada, *Studi Francesi*, VIII (1959), 288.
.2   G. Muraille, *Cahiers de Civilisation Médiévale*, II (1959), 478.

191   —, 'Une Edition nouvelle des *Lais* de Marie de France', *Romance Philology*, XXII (1968-9), 600-13.
Reviews favourably the edition by Jean Rychner (item 13) and contributes a large number of important observations on the text of the *Lais*.

192   —, 'Remarques sur la structure du lai, essai de définition et de classement', in *La Littérature narrative d'imagination, des genres littéraires aux techniques d'expression* (Colloque de Strasbourg, 23-25 avril, 1959). Paris: Presses Universitaires de France, 1961, pp. 23-39.
General remarks of considerable interest. Stresses the importance of the Other World in the structure of the *lai* and the role of *aventure*, which links a 'monde terrestre, banal, vulgaire, quotidien' to a 'monde supérieur, idéal'.
Review by:
.1   F. Lecoy, *Romania*, LXXXIII (1962), 429-30.

193   Frey, John A. 'Linguistic and Psychological Couplings in the Lays of Marie de France', *Studies in Philology*, LXI (1964), 3-18.
Coupling is seen as a fundamental stylistic and organizing principle in

the *Lais,* in accordance with the courtly ideal of creating harmonious balances. Various types of couplings are found, the octosyllabic couplets, the stress on love as a mutual passion, symbolic couplings (e.g. Guigemar's love which cures both his physical and his spiritual wound), linguistic couplings (the use of qualifying adjectives, groupings of qualities), etc. The *Lais* are divided into three groups on the basis of the creation and dissolution of couplings. The article contains some useful observations, but the case is often overstated. See item 375.
Review by:

.1   S. Cigada, *Studi Francesi,* XXVII (1966), 116.

194   Freymond, E. 'Altfranzösisches Kunstepos und Romane', *Kritischer Jahresbericht über die Fortschritte der romanischen Philologie,* III (1891-4), 2nd part, 140-94.
Contains a section entitled 'Die *Lais bretons* und Marie de France' (pp. 163-7). A review of recent work, in particular Ahlström (item 77).

195   — , 'Über den reichen Reim bei altfranzösischen Dichtern bis zum Anfang des XIV. Jahrh.', *Zeitschrift für romanische Philologie,* VI (1882), 1-36, 177-215.
The results of the enquiry for Marie's *Lais* and *Fables* are found on pp. 22-3.

196   Fuchs, Walter. *Der Tristanroman und die höfische Liebes-novelle.* Rohrschach: Lehner, 1967.
Marie's *Lais* are discussed on pp. 14-32.

197   Gallais, Pierre. 'Recherches sur la mentalité des romanciers français du moyen âge' *Cahiers de Civilisation Médiévale,* VII (1964), 479-93; XIII (1970), 333-47.
Contains a number of isolated references to Marie.

198   Galliot, Marcel. *Etudes d'ancien français, moyen âge et XVIe siècle: licence, CAPES, agrégation.* Brussels, Paris & Montreal: Didier, 1967.
Contains an elementary study of the language of *Lanval,* ll. 237-74 (pp. 140-9) and of *Eliduc,* ll. 29-63 (pp. 150-7).

199   Gennrich, Friedrich. 'Zwei altfranzösische *Lais*', *Studi Medievali,* new series, XV (1942), 1-68. Also in separate print, Turin: Chiantore, 1942.
Contains a transcription of the *Lai du Chievrefueil* (pp. 39 ff.).

200   Golther, Wolfgang. *Tristan und Isolde in den Dichtungen des Mittelalters und der neuen Zeit.* Leipzig: Hirzel, 1907.
Contains comments on *Chevrefoil* (pp. 221-3).

201 —, *Tristan und Isolde in der französischen und deutschen Dichtung des Mittelalters und der Neuzeit.* Berlin and Leipzig: Walter de Gruyter, 1929.

Chevrefoil is discussed on pp. 43-4.

202 Gourmont, Remy de. *Promenades littéraires.* 6 vols, Paris: Mercure de France, 1904-27.

Vol. II, pp. 237-47, contains an appreciation of the adaptations of Marie's *Lais* by Jean Moréas (item 61) and vol. V, pp. 196-206, a chapter entitled 'Marie de France et les contes de fées'.

203 Green, Robert B. '*Fin'amors* dans deux lais de Marie de France: *Equitan* et *Chaitivel*', *Le Moyen Age*, LXXXI (1975), 265-72.

Equitan and *Chaitivel* are united in their rejection of the ideal of courtly love. They establish the philosophical basis of the other *lais*, warning us of the dangers of lust and lack of commitment in love.

204 —, 'The Fusion of Magic and Realism in two Lays of Marie de France', *Neophilologus*, LIX (1975), 324-36.

A thorough and perceptive study of *Guigemar* and *Milun*, which are seen as treating the same theme, responsibility and commitment in love. The principal obstacles to harmony and fulfilment are the states of mind and emotional immaturity of the characters themselves. The prison in which Guigemar's lady is kept is a projection of the lack of tenderness and commitment in her experience of love. Her love for Guigemar enables her to leave the garden and to follow him across the sea, symbol of birth and life. In *Milun* permanent union between the parents will only be achieved after Milun's successful quest for his son, born from an irresponsible relationship and rejected by his parents. The swan is a phallic symbol representing the carnal nature of the union between Milun and his lady. The contradictions in the story suggest that Milun is the lady's husband, for once atonement has been made for the rejection of the son, the swan and the lady's husband disappear from the text.

205 —, 'Marie de France's *Laüstic*: Love's Victory through Symbolic Expression', *Romance Notes*, XVI (1974-5), 695-9.

An examination of the symbolism of *Laüstic* indicates that the poem does not recount the consequences of an unhappy love affair, but rather the sublimation of a relationship which triumphs over external limitations. The room, symbolic of the sterile relationship between the lady and her husband, is a feminine symbol, which is replaced by the masculine image of the nightingale. At the close of the poem the dead bird in the jewel case (the author points to Freud's link between a jewel case and the female genital organ) represents the permanent physical union of the lovers, a union which will flourish and triumph over the husband's anger and neglect of his wife.

206   Grimes, E. Margaret. *The Lays of Desiré, Graelent and Melion: Edition of the Texts with an Introduction.* New York: Institute of French Studies, 1928.
Frequent references to Marie in introduction, in particular to *Lanval* and *Bisclavret*.

207   Gröber, Gustav. *Grundriss der romanischen Philologie.* 2 vols, Strasbourg: Trübner, 1888-1902; 2nd ed. 1904-6.
Volume II contains some often quoted remarks on Marie's works (*Lais*, pp. 594-7; *Fables*, pp. 632-3; *Espurgatoire*, p. 641).

208   Hanoset, Micheline. 'Des origines de la *matière de Bretagne*, II: La légende arthurienne: Chrétien de Troyes et Marie de France', *Marche Romane*, X (1960), 67-77.
Evidence from Marie is discussed with reference to the continental or insular transmission of Celtic tales (pp. 72-5).

209   Haskins, Charles H. 'Henry II as a Patron of Literature', in *Essays in Medieval History Presented to Thomas Frederick Tout.* Manchester, 1925, pp. 71-7.
Presents a list of twenty works which were definitely or possibly dedicated to Henry II. Marie's *Lais* figure under no. 16.

210   Hatcher, Anna G. 'Lai du *Chievrefueil*, 61-78; 107-13', *Romania*, LXXI (1950), 330-44.
Supports Spitzer's idea (item 424) of a 'message unwritten but divined'. This idea of the miracle of love's understanding alone gives coherence to the expression *Ceo fu la sume de l'escrit*. Spitzer's view of ll. 107-13 is, however, unacceptable. The term *paroles* in l. 111 must refer to the message, not to Iseut's words at the time of the lovers' meeting. Logic and poetic sense require this.

211   Hatzfeld, Helmut A. 'Esthetic Criticism Applied to Medieval Romance Literature', *Romance Philology*, I (1947-8), 305-27.
Marie is the subject of pp. 319-20. Principally a discussion of Spitzer's views.

212   Hertz, Wilhelm. *Der Werwolf: Beitrag zur Sagengeschichte.* Stuttgart, 1862.
Contains remarks on *Bisclavret* (pp. 90-3).

213   Hervieux, Léopold. *Les Fabulistes latins, depuis le siècle*

d'Auguste jusqu'à la fin du moyen âge. 2 vols, Paris: Firmin-Didot, 1884; 2nd ed., 5 vols, 1883-9.
Contains a substantial section on Marie de France (2nd ed., vol. I, pp. 730-63), dealing with biographical details, the *Fables* and the manuscripts of the *Fables.* Accepts that Marie worked directly from an English collection of fables and supports La Rue's identification of *le cunte Willame* as William Longsword (see items 279 and 280). Important changes in second edition as a result of the review by G. Paris. Review by:

.1   G. Paris, *Journal des Savants,* 1884, pp. 670-86; 1885, pp. 37-51.

214   Hirsh, John C. 'Providential Concern in the *Lay Le Freine',* *Notes and Queries,* new series, XVI (1969), 85-6.
Concerns the relationship between *Le Fresne* and the Middle English romance *Lay le Freine.*

215   Hoepffner, Ernest. 'The Breton *Lais',* in *Arthurian Literature in the Middle Ages: a Collaborative History,* edited by Roger Sherman Loomis. Oxford: Clarendon Press, 1959, pp. 112-21.
Only *Lanval* and *Chevrefoil* are accepted as Arthurian *lais.*

216   —, 'Pour la chronologie des *Lais* de Marie de France', *Romania,* LIX (1933), 351-70; LX (1934), 36-66.
Lanval and *Yonec* are thematically a diptych and both are influenced by the *Roman de Brut* and the *Roman de Thèbes. Guigemar* shows less influence from these two romances, but this lay is indebted, particularly in its first part, to the *Roman d'Eneas.* The evidence suggests that *Lanval* and *Yonec* were composed at approximately the same time, perhaps shortly after the *Brut,* around 1160, and that *Guigemar* was written somewhat later. An interesting and detailed study. See item 242.

217   —, 'Les Deux Lais du *Chèvrefeuille',* in *Mélanges de littérature, d'histoire et de philologie offerts à Paul Laumonier.* Paris: Droz, 1935, pp. 41-9. Reprint, Geneva: Slatkine, 1972.
On the relationship between Marie's *Chevrefoil* and the lyric poem, the *Lai du Chievrefeuil.* The author of the latter must have drawn his title and the general content of his poem from Marie, which indicates that she influenced lyric poetry as well as the romance.

218   —, 'La Géographie et l'histoire dans les *Lais* de Marie de France', *Romania,* LVI (1930), 1-32.
An important and detailed article. In a discussion of their origins the *Lais* should not all be categorized under the same heading. Marie's localization is not always a sign of the country of origin. Some geographical references are preserved from the original, but in several lays

Marie has imposed her own localization (*Bisclavret, Laüstic, Chaitivel, Fresne, Lanval* and probably *Eliduc*). There has been a visible effort to impart to the lays an historical character. All except *Chaitivel* and *Laüstic* are situated in the distant past. This legendary atmosphere is created by the use of geographical and historical indications, almost all of which derive not from Marie's source but from the *Brut* of Wace.

219   —, 'Graëlent ou Lanval?', in *Recueil de travaux offert à M. Clovis Brunel.* Paris: Société de l'Ecole des Chartes (Mémoires et Documents, XII), 1955, vol. II, pp. 1-8.
Chrétien's *Erec* (ed. Roques, ll. 1902ff.) indicates that legends of Graelent Muer and Guingamor existed by 1170. Marie took the story of Graelent, substituted the name Lanval and gave the tale an Arthurian setting. The extant *Graelent* is more faithful to the original story.

220   —, 'Le Lai d'*Equitan* de Marie de France', in *A Miscellany of Studies in Romance Languages and Literatures Presented to Leon E. Kastner.* Cambridge: Cambridge University Press, 1932, pp. 294-302.
Equitan can be divided into two contrasting parts, ll. 1-184 (ed. Ewert; ll. 1-188, ed. Warnke) stemming from Marie's imagination, and ll. 185-314 corresponding to a primitive tale suitable for a *fabliau* or a 'conte drolatique'. Although the first part of the text betrays knowledge of the *Eneas*, the principal influence here is the Provençal code of love. The interest in Provençal theories seems to mark the last stage of Marie's evolution, and *Equitan* is probably Marie's last lay.

221   —, *Les Lais de Marie de France.* Paris: Boivin (Bibliothèque de la Revue des Cours et Conférences), 1935, 179pp. Reprint, Paris: Nizet, 1966.
An important synthesis. Introductory studies (I, Les Origines; II, Le *Roman de Thèbes;* III, Le *Brut* de Wace; IV, Contes et lais bretons) are followed by biographical details relating to Marie (pp. 49-55) and a useful, if somewhat dated, analysis of each of the *lais*. The *nobles reis* is seen as Henry II (p. 51) and count William, hesitantly, as William Longsword. Most, if not all, the *lais* were composed by 1167 (p. 55). Reviews by:
.1   W. Küchler, *Literaturblatt für germanische und romanische Philologie,* LVIII (1937), cols 265-8.
.2   K. Lewent, *Archivum Romanicum,* XXIII (1939), 344-50.

222   —, 'Les *Lais* de Marie de France dans *Galeran de Bretagne* et *Guillaume de Dole*', *Romania,* LVI (1930), 212-35.
Galeran de Bretagne and *Guillaume de Dole* follow closely Marie's *Le Fresne* and *Lanval* respectively, but one cannot speak of plagiarism. In

addition, although similar principles of adaptation are employed, the evidence suggests that *Galeran* and *Guillaume* were not composed by the same author. See item 471.

223 —, 'Marie de France et l'*Eneas*', *Studi Medievali,* new series, V (1932), 272-308.
There is no trace of *Eneas* in *Yonec* or *Laüstic.* In other *lais* there are isolated reminiscences, the most significant of which is found in *Milun,* where the exchange of messages between the two lovers recalls that between Aeneas and Lavinia. However, in *Guigemar, Eliduc* and *Equitan* the influence of *Eneas* is incontestable. This suggests that these three *lais* were composed later than *Lanval,* in which, atypically, there is no discernible contact with *Eneas.* See items 298, 397, and 398.

224 —, 'Marie de France et les lais anonymes', *Studi Medievali,* new series, IV (1931), 1-31.
Discusses the attribution of *Guingamor* and *Tydorel* to Marie. The former was probably not composed by her. In the case of *Tydorel* one can reject the attribution to Marie with greater certainty.

225 —, *Aux origines de la nouvelle française.* Oxford: Clarendon Press, 1939(The Taylorian Lectures, 1938).
A general introduction to the *Lais.* Useful remarks on symbols, pp. 19 and 35ff.

226 —, 'Le Roman d'*Ille et Galeron* et le lai d'*Eliduc*', in *Studies in French Language and Mediæval Literature Presented to Professor Mildred K. Pope.* Manchester: Manchester University Press (Publications of the University of Manchester, CCLXVIII), 1939, pp. 125-44.
Gautier's aim was to provide an improved version of *Eliduc* and to make his characters morally and socially perfect. He was thus an imitator and profound critic of Marie. The way in which Gautier speaks in the prologue of the coronation in 1167 of Beatrice, wife of Frederick Barbarossa, suggests that the romance was begun not long after this date. *Eliduc* must therefore have existed by 1170, perhaps by 1167-8.

227 —, 'Thomas d'Angleterre et Marie de France', *Studi Medievali,* new series, VII (1934), 8-23.
Marie's *Lais* were composed before the *Tristan* of Thomas. The latter was influenced not only by the text of certain *lais* (a number of parallels, often unconvincing, are put forward), but also by her 'art simple et gracieux'.

228 —, 'La Tradition manuscrite des *Lais* de Marie de France',

Neophilologus, XII (1927), 1-10, 85-96.

Concludes that MSS H and S represent 'les deux extrémités de la chaîne dont les copies secondaires, P, Q et C, forment les anneaux intermédiaires' (p. 95). There seem to have been from an early period two different versions of the *Lais,* an insular version, represented by H and C, and a continental version, represented by S, P and Q. The Anglo-Norman manuscripts are closer to the original than the continental manuscripts. See items 115 and 413.

229   Hofer, Stefan. 'Zur Beurteilung der *Lais* der Marie de France', *Zeitschrift für romanische Philologie,* LXVI (1950), 409-21.
Gaimar's *Estoire des Engleis* (ed. Bell, ll. 3737ff.) is seen as an important source of *Equitan,* and traces of the Tristan legend are found in several *lais.*

230   —, 'Der *Tristanroman* und der *Lai du Chievrefueil* der Marie de France', *Zeitschrift für romanische Philologie,* LXIX (1953), 129-31.
Marie composed her *lai* from hints found in earlier Tristan texts. Review by:
.1   A. Goosse, *Les Lettres Romanes,* XI (1957), 318.

231   Holmes, Urban T., Jr. *Daily Living in the Twelfth Century, Based on the Observations of Alexander Neckam in London and Paris.* Madison: Univ. of Wisconsin Press, 1952.
Marie's works are used as a source of supplementary information some dozen times.

232   —, 'Further on Marie de France', *Symposium,* III (1949), 335-9.
Marie shows little awareness in *Eliduc* and *Le Fresne* of the decisions of Pope Alexander III governing marriage and divorce. Entry into religion by a partner does not permit the dissolution of a marriage. Thus Guilliadun and Eliduc marry in violation of Canon law. The marriage between Gurun and La Codre could only have been annulled if Gurun had committed adultery with Le Fresne after his exchange of vows with La Codre. If Marie were Abbess of Shaftesbury (see items 183 and 184) it is unlikely that she would have evinced a lack of concern for correct procedure in such matters.

233   —, *A History of Old French Literature from the Origins to 1300.* New York: Crofts, 1937 Revised ed., New York: Russell and Russell, 1962.
Offers a good introduction to the *Lais* and to the biographical problems surrounding Marie (pp. 185-92). For the *Fables* see pp. 207-10. Marie, it

is suggested, was the daughter of Waleran de Meulan and as a result of her marriage to Hugh Talbot may have lived in Hereford (then in Wales) and Devon. Hereford was the scene of a literary renaissance towards the end of the twelfth century. See items 172, 173, 232, 234, 236 and 467

234 —, 'New Thoughts on Marie de France', *Studies in Philology*, XXIX (1932), 1-10.

Useful summary of the theories concerning the identity of Marie followed by an attempt at identification as 'Marie, eighth child of Galeran de Meulan, a Norman noble with his fief in the French Vexin, and of Agnes de Montfort'. This Marie married Hugh Talbot, Baron of Cleuville, who owned lands in Hereford and Buckinghamshire. Cleuville is perhaps Clovelly in North Devon, on Barnstaple Bay, belonging to Walter of Claville. An alliance between Walter and the Talbot family is 'entirely possible'. See items 172, 173 and 465.

235 —, 'Old French *Yonec*', *Modern Philology*, XXIX (1931-2), 225-9.

A suggestion that the name Yonec is connected with his mission as comforter ('Icil [la] recunforterat; / Yonec numer le f[e]rat', 329-30). The etymology may thus be a Breton formation *dihudennêc,* 'a comforting individual'.

236 —, A Welsh Motif in Marie's *Guigemar*', *Studies in Philology*, XXXIX (1942), 11-14.

As the wife of Hugh Talbot (see items 234 and 467), Marie would have resided in Hereford on the Welsh border. She may have heard the tale recounted by Giraldus Cambrensis of the killing of a hind with male antlers, resulting in the loss of sight in the right eye and a lingering illness for the hunter responsible. The introductory motif in *Guigemar* may well be modelled on this incident, which took place not far from Radnor. The *braz de mer* mentioned by Marie (l. 150) could be the Severn seen from the hills above Monmouth and reached through the Golden Valley of the Wye.

237 Honeycutt, Benjamin L. 'Computer Generated Concordances to the *Lais* and the *Fabliaux*: Format, Problems, and Potential', in *The Study of French Literature with Computers*, ed. John R. Allen. Winnipeg: The University of Manitoba, 1973, pp. 5-16.

An account of the completed concordance to the *fabliaux* and to *Laüstic* and of the projected concordance to the *Lais,* which will include the concordance proper, a word frequency list and a morphological index.

238   —, 'The Interaction of Structure, Description and Symbol
       in *Yonec* of Marie de France', *The University of South
       Florida Language Quarterly,* XII (1974), 24-5, 28.
       Yonec contains three structural levels, request (ll. 91-104), prophecy
       (ll. 209-10, 327-32) and fulfilment (ll. 127-30, 319-22, 545-6). This
       structural unity is complemented by the manipulation of description
       and symbol, with physical description reflecting the lady's mental state.
       The symbolic tower changes its nature: beginning as a prison, it becomes
       a haven (ll. 217-18) and finally it is again connected with sorrow.

239   Hunt, Tony. 'Glossing Marie de France', *Romanische
       Forschungen,* LXXXVI (1974), 396-418.
       A penetrating study of the interpretative problems raised by the
       Prologue to the *Lais.* In opposition to Spitzer (item 426) and Robertson
       (item 386), Hunt does not think that Marie is referring in ll. 15-16 to
       the technique of scriptural exegesis. The Prologue is seen as a reflection
       of twelfth-century humanist thought, in particular the idea of the
       continuity of study and progress.

240   Illingworth, R.N. 'Celtic Tradition and the *Lai* of *Guigemar*',
       Medium Aevum, XXXI (1962), 176-87.
       Guigemar represents a combination of two distinct themes with dia-
       metrically opposed characteristics: (1) an all-powerful fairy lures a
       chosen mortal to her fairy island (27-534); (2) a lady is held against her
       will by an amorous knight and rescued by her lover (693-882). Both
       themes derive from the common Celtic stock of story material. An Irish
       nucleus was transmitted to Wales and thence to Brittany where it was
       modified and later adapted by Marie under the influence of Old French
       literary fashions.
       Review by:
  .1   G. Favati, *Studi Francesi,* XX (1963), 323-4.

241   —, 'Celtic Tradition and the *lai* of *Yonec*', *Etudes Celtiques,*
       IX (1960-1), 501-20.
       Yonec consists of two themes: (a) the story of a mortal lady who is
       visited by a supernatural lover in the form of a bird; (b) the story of a
       son who is born after the death of his father and who subsequently kills
       his father's murderer. Both themes existed separately in Irish literature
       before the date of composition of *Yonec,* which suggests that the *lai*
       derives from Celtic sources. See items 138, 253 and 344.

242   —, 'La Chronologie des *Lais* de Marie de France', *Romania,*
       LXXXVII (1966), 433-75.
       An important study in which the *Lais* are divided on the basis of nomen-

clature, internal stylistic similarities and literary borrowings into two
groups. *Bisclavret, Le Fresne, Laüstic, Chaitivel, Deus Amanz* and
Equitan show the influence of the *Estoire des Engleis* and the *Brut*
(Deus Amanz and *Equitan* also betray signs of borrowing from *Piramus
et Thisbé)* and were probably composed between 1155 and 1160.
Lanval, Yonec, Milun, Chevrefoil, Guigemar and *Eliduc* suggest that
Marie had read *Eneas* and an early version of the Tristan legend and
were composed between 1160 and 1165. Certainly the entire collection
including the Prologue was composed before 1170. See item 216.

243   —, ' The Composition of *Graelent* and *Guingamor*', *Medium
       Aevum,* XLIV (1975), 31-50.
       Supports Segre's view (item 413) that the three *lais* were composed in
       the order *Lanval, Graelent, Guingamor,* but suggests that it is necessary
       to expose the Celtic traditions in *Graelent* and *Guingamor* in order to
       understand their relationship to Marie's *lais* and to each other. Con-
       cludes that both *Graelent* and *Guingamor* drew extensively on Marie's
       lais, in particular on *Lanval,* but that *Guingamor* also drew material from
       Graelent. Both *Graelent* and *Guingamor* 'contain a nucleus of genuine
       Celtic tradition quite independent of *Lanval*'.

244   Jacobs, Joseph. *The Fables of Aesop as first printed by
       William Caxton in 1484 with those of Avian, Alfonso and
       Poggio.* 2 vols, London: Nutt, 1889.
       Vol. I ('History of the Aesopic Fable') contains a study of Marie's
       Fables (pp. 159-72), claiming that they must derive from an Arabic
       Aesop and that the Alfred mentioned by Marie is Alfred the Englishman
       referred to by Roger Bacon in his *Compendium studii.*
       Review by:
  .1   L. Sudre, *Romania,* XX (1891), 289-97.

245   Jauss, Hans R. *Untersuchungen zur mittelalterlichen Tierdich-
       tung.* Tübingen: Niemeyer (Beihefte zur *Zeitschrift für
       romanische Philologie,* C), 1959, 314 pp.
       Contains substantial material on the *Fables* (esp. pp. 24-55), which are
       seen as a parody of the contemporary courtly romance.

246   Jauss, Hans R. and Erich Köhler (ed.). *Grundriss der roman-
       ischen Literaturen des Mittelalters,* vol I., *Généralités,* ed.
       Maurice Delbouille, Heidelberg: Winter, 1972.
       Offers important general material relevant to Marie de France.

247   Jeanroy, Alfred. 'Les *Lais* de Marie de France', in *Histoire de
       la nation française,* ed. G. Hanotaux. Paris: Plon, 1920-4, vol.
       XII (1921), pt. I, pp. 283-7.
       General introduction.

248 —, 'Marie de France', in *La Grande Encyclopédie: inventaire raisonné des sciences, des lettres et des arts.* 31 vols, Paris; 1885-1901, vol. XXIII (n.d.), p. 112.
General introduction.

249 Jodogne, Omer. 'L'Autre Monde celtique dans la littérature française du XIIe siècle', *Bulletin de la Classe des Lettres et des Sciences Morales et Politiques de l'Académie Royale de Belgique,* 5th series, XLVI (1960), 584-97.
Contains some useful remarks on the *merveilleux* element in the *Lais.*

250 —, 'L'Interprétation des textes médiévaux', *Les Lettres Romanes,* VII (1953), 369-70.
A note arising from P. Le Gentil's article on *Chevrefoil* (item 289) and stressing the importance of the symbolic interpretation of medieval texts.

251 Johnston, Grahame. 'Chaucer and the Breton Lays', in *Proceedings and Papers of the Fourteenth Congress of the Australasian Universities Language and Literature Association,* ed. K.I.D. Maslen. Dunedin, New Zealand, 1972, pp. 230-41.
A discussion of the relationship between the Middle English Breton lays, including Chaucer's *Franklin's Tale,* and the poems of Marie, which are seen as the 'norm of the literary Breton *lai'.*

252 Johnston, Oliver M. 'Sources of the Lay of the *Two Lovers',* *Modern Language Notes,* XXI (1906), 34-9.
Marie's *Deus Amanz* is derived from two closely related groups of stories: (a) A father loses his wife and wishes to marry his own daughter; (b) A marriage is conditioned by the performance of some difficult task. These two themes were combined by Marie's predecessor, a minstrel or story-teller.

253 —, 'Sources of the Lay of *Yonec', Publications of the Modern Language Association of America,* XX (1905), 322-38.
Yonec represents the fusion of two cycles of stories from different sources, the *Inclusa* theme, which is probably oriental, and the Jealous Stepmother theme, which is Western, probably Celtic. See items 138, 241 and 344.

254 —, 'The Story of the Blue Bird and the Lay of *Yonec',Studi Medievali,* II (1906-7), 1-10.
Most of the important incidents in Blue Bird and *Yonec* are different. Each tale is composed of two independent stories. In *Yonec* the theme

of the *Inclusa* is combined with the tale of the Jealous Stepmother. In Blue Bird the Jealous Stepmother theme is linked to the cycle of stories connected with *La Belle et la Bête.*

255 Johnston, Ronald C. 'Sound-Related Couplets in Old French', *Forum for Modern Language Studies,* XII (1976), 194-205.
Marie's attitude in the *Fables* towards the linking of couplets by sound is examined on pp. 201-2.

256 Joly, Aristide. *Marie de France et les fables au moyen-âge.* Paris: Durand, 1863, 65pp. Extrait des Mémoires de l'Académie des Sciences, Arts et Belles-Lettres de Caen, 1863, pp. 415-77.

257 Jones, Rosemarie. *The Theme of Love in the Romans d'Antiquité.* London: The Modern Humanities Research Association (Dissertation Series, V), 1972.
Contains a chapter entitled 'Marie de France and the *Romans d'Antiquité'* (pp. 71-6). Concludes that 'Marie is indebted to or influenced by the *romans antiques* to a greater extent than has yet been suspected; influenced not only textually, but also by the concepts underlying the *romans antiques'.* Some interesting remarks on Marie's vocabulary.

258 Jubainville, H. d'Arbois de. *'Lai',* Romania, VIII (1879), 422-5.
Remarks on the Irish origin of the term *lai.*

259 Kamber, Gerald. 'A Case of Symbolic Syntax in the *Chievrefueil',* Romance Notes, I (1959-60), 151-4.
An unconvincing analysis of ll. 77-8 ('Bele amie, si est de nus: / Ne vus sanz mei, ne mei sanz vus! '). The words themselves are seen as the symbol of the union between Tristan and Iseut.

260 Keidel, George C. 'The History of French Fable Manuscripts', *Publications of the Modern Language Association of America,* XXIV (1909), 207-19.
Offers an account of the twenty-four extant MSS of Marie's *Fables* (pp. 208-12). Marie's collection of fables seems to have been the most popular of all in the Middle Ages.

261 Kelemina, Jakob. *Geschichte der Tristansage nach den Dichtungen des Mittelalters.* Vienna: Hölzel, 1923.
Chevrefoil is discussed on pp. 157-9.

262 Kemp-Welch, Alice. *Of Six Mediaeval Women.* London: Mac-

millan, 1913.
Chapter II is entitled 'A Twelfth-Century Romance Writer, Marie de France' (pp. 29-56). A good general introduction to Marie with interesting material on symbolism and folk-lore elements in the *Lais.*

263   Keyser, R.and C.R. Unger. *Strengleikar eda Lioðabok.* Christiania: Feilberg & Landmark, 1850.
An edition of the thirteenth-century Norse translation of *lais* by Marie and others. Contains Marie's Prologue, *Guigemar, Le Fresne, Equitan, Bisclavret, Laüstic, Chaitivel* (from l. 85), *Deus Amanz, Milun, Chevrefoil, Lanval* (from l. 155) and *Yonec.* See items 85 (pp. 50-3) and 416.

264   Kingsford, Charles L. *The Song of Lewes.* Oxford: Clarendon Press, 1890.
Contains a description of MS Harley 978 with a detailed list of its contents (pp. vii-xviii).

265   Kittredge, G.L. *'Arthur and Gorlagon', Harvard Studies and Notes in Philology and Literature,* VIII (1903), 149-275.
A detailed study of a number of werewolf stories. *Bisclavret* is discussed in relation to *Arthur and Gorlagon,* the *Lai de Melion,* the Irish story of The Fairy Wife, etc.
Review by:
.1   H. d'Arbois de Jubainville, *Revue Celtique,* XXIV (1903), 324-5.

266   — , *'Launfal', American Journal of Philology,* X (1889), 1-33.
The text of the Rawlinson version of *Launfal.* The introduction contains numerous references to *Lanval* and *Graelent.*

267   Klingender, Francis. *Animals in Art and Thought to the End of the Middle Ages,* London: Routledge and Kegan Paul, 1971.
Refers to *Fables* (p. 360) and *Guigemar* (p. 482). Provides a wealth of artistic and literary analogues for the presentation of animals in Marie's works.

268   Knapton, Antoinette. *Mythe et psychologie chez Marie de France dans Guigemar.* Chapel Hill: Univ. of North Carolina Press (North Carolina Studies in the Romance Languages and Literatures, CXLII), 1975, 145pp.
Contains three main chapters: (1) 'Mythe et Psychologie', (2) 'Explication textuelle et symbolique', (3) 'Le *sen'.* The analysis follows the text closely and discusses in particular the symbolic motifs used, the white hart, the magic boat, the love belt and knot, etc., which are traced to their Celtic, classical and biblical sources. A published version of item 495.

269 —, 'La Poésie enluminée de Marie de France', *Romance Philology*, XXX (1976-7), 177-87.

A suggestive examination of colour terms in Marie. Six colours are used: gold, green, white, *vermeil, bis* and *purpre*. Marie's use of these colours, which correspond to those employed by the Church for priestly vestments and altar ornaments, is discreet but significant. The *lais* which are most affected are *Guigemar, Lanval* and *Yonec,* those often called 'lais féeriques'. The choice of colours indicates that Marie's upbringing was either cloistered or at least exposed constantly to ecclesiastical ritual. One possible 'Marie' is Marie de Boulogne, daughter of Stephen of England and Mathilda of Boulogne. Like Le Fresne this Marie was raised in a convent and left it to marry, in 1161. Her husband was Matthew de Warren, son of the count of Flanders.

270 Kolls, A. *Zur Lanvalsage: eine Quellenuntersuchung.* Berlin: Hettler, 1886, 72pp.

Studies mainly the English versions of the story, but demonstrates the link between *Graelent* and *Lanval,* quoting 75 parallel passages. The evidence suggests a common source and rules out the possibility of single authorship or the direct derivation of one lay from the other. Review by:

.1 G. Paris, *Romania,* XV (1886), 644.

271 Koubichkine, Michèle. 'A Propos du *Lai de Lanval'*, *Le Moyen Age,* LXXVIII (1972), 467-88.

A penetrating study of the text of *Lanval* aimed at discovering the meaning of the hero's name. Alienated from the world of the Arthurian court, Lanval finds his true essence when he follows his mistress to the Other World. His flight to Avalon is at the same time a discovery of his own identity, his own name (cf. MS C, *Launval*) being a virtual anagram of the form *Avalun* (l. 641).
Review by:

.1 G. Di Stefano, *Studi Francesi,* LI (1973), 520.

272 Krappe, Alexander H. *Balor with the Evil Eye: Studies in Celtic and French Literature.* New York: Columbia University, Institut des Etudes Françaises, 1927.

Chapter I deals with the lay of *Yonec,* which is seen as a Christian and courtly version of the Irish myth of Balor, the robber on Tory Island on the North-East coast of Ireland. This legend was adapted to the civilisation of France and England and at the same time contaminated with the tale of the Jealous Stepmother.

273 —, 'The Vassal of the Devil', *Archivum Romanicum,* VII

(1923), 470-7.

Marie's fable *De fure et sortilega* (ed. Warnke, no. XLVIII) is the earliest extant version of an Anglo-Saxon legend of the devil and his vassal, a legend of pagan origin. In this article it is compared in particular with the forty-fifth story of *El conde Lucanor* of Don Juan Manuel.

274   Küchler,Walther, 'Schön Annie, Fraisne und Griselda', *Die neueren Sprachen*, XXXV (1927), 489-97.
Discusses the relationship between *Le Fresne,* Boccaccio's tale of Griselda and the Scottish ballads of Fair Annie, the earliest of which date from the sixteenth century.

275   La Croix du Maine (Francois Grudé, sire de la Croix, *dit*). *Premier volume de la Bibliothèque du sieur de La Croix Du Maine, qui est un catalogue général de toutes sortes d'autheurs qui ont escrit en françois depuis cinq cents ans et plus,jusques à ce jour d'huy.* Paris, 1584.
Contains a reference to 'Marie de France, damoiselle Françoise, for bien versee en la poësie usitee de son temps, sçavoir en l'an de salut 1260, ou environ. Elle a mis en vers François les Fables d'Esope Moralisées, lesquelles elle a traduites de langue Angloise, en la nostre Françoise, comme tesmoigne Claude Fauchet en son recueil des Poëtes' (p. 310). Offers the first attempt to provide a precise date for Marie's literary activity. See item 276 and Baum, item 85, p. 62.

276   La Croix du Maine, François Grudé de and Antoine Du Verdier. *Les Bibliothéques françoises de La Croix-Dumaine et de Du Verdier.* 6 vols, Paris, 1772-3.
A reprint of items 275 and 160. For comments on Marie see vol. II, p. 89 (La Croix du Maine) and vol. V, p. 23 (Du Verdier). Neither author seems aware of the existence of the *Lais.*

277   Lakits, Pál. *La Châtelaine de Vergi et l'évolution de la nou-velle courtoise.*Debrecen: Kossuth Lajos Tudományegyetem (Studia Romanica Universitatis Debreceniensis de Ludovico Kossuth Nominatae, II), 1966, 114pp.
Contains frequent references to Marie's *Lais,* in particular to *Lanval.* Excellent material on a number of thematic aspects of the *Lais.*

278   *La Mée, K.W. *A Metrical Study of Five Lais of Marie de France.* The Hague: Mouton, 1974. See item 496.

279   La Rue, Gervais de. 'Dissertation on the Life and Writings of Mary, an Anglo-Norman Poetess of the 13th Century', *Archaeologia,* XIII (1800), 35-67. Extract in item 91.
The first substantial presentation of Marie in English. Discusses the

Harley collection of *lais* (seen as dedicated to Henry III, possibly to Louis VIII or St Louis), the *Fables* (Count William is identified as William Longsword, an interpretation accepted by many later scholars) and the *Espurgatoire* (pp. 65-6). Article still of considerable interest. See Baum, item 85, pp. 80-3.

280   —, *Essais historiques sur les bardes, les jongleurs et les trouvères normands et anglo-normands.* 3 vols, Caen: Mancel, 1834.

Marie is discussed in vol. III, pp. 47-100. She was probably born in Normandy, perhaps in Brittany, where she may have belonged to one of the Breton families with fiefs in England. The *Lais* were probably dedicated to Henry III of England, possibly to Louis VIII of France. The count mentioned in the *Fables* must be English, probably William Longsword.

281   —, *Recherches sur les ouvrages des bardes de la Bretagne armoricaine dans le moyen âge.* Caen: Poisson, 1815.

Marie is discussed on pp. 11-14. The king to whom the *Lais* are dedicated appears to be Henry III.

282   La Serna Santander, Carlos Antonio de. *Mémoire historique sur la Bibliothèque dite de Bourgogne, présentement Bibliothèque publique de Bruxelles.* Brussels, 1809.

Marie de France is discussed on pp. 5-8. Count William is identified as Guillaume de Dampierre. Marie was born in France, but brought up in Flanders. Mentions the *Espurgatoire*, but not the *Lais*.

283   Laurie, Helen C.R. 'A Note on the Composition of Marie's *Guigemar'*, *Medium Aevum*, XLIV (1975), 242-8.

If the *aventure* recounted by Marie stems from oral tradition, Marie is often leaning on the *lettre* of other poets (e.g., *Eneas, Thèbes, Cligès*, etc.). Line 23 ('Sulunc la lettre e l'escriture') refers to Marie's literary models, which she refashions. 'Marie has shaped the amorphous matter through an experience of faithful love, which is her own structural device, and like her fellow poets is improving on the *auctores* by the romantic expression of feeling'.

284   Lawton, H.W. *'L'uevre Salemon'*, *Modern Language Review*, L (1955), 50-2.

The expression *l'uevre Salemon* was probably derived from *opus Salomonis*, which is attested on several occasions in the Vulgate. Solomon's chief work is the Temple, whose wonders and marvellous workmanship may well be reflected in the use of the phrase *l'uevre Salemon* in Old French texts. See items 72, 81, 114 and 466.

285   Lazar, Moshé. *Amour courtois et fin'amors dans la littérature
       du XIIe siècle.* Paris: Klincksieck (Bibliothèque Française et
       Romane, série C, Etudes Littéraires, VIII), 1964.
       Contains a substantial section on the *Lais* (pp. 174-98), stressing Marie's
       personal role in the 'transformation morale' which took place during the
       years 1150-65.

286   Leach, Henry G. *Angevin Britain and Scandinavia.* Cambridge,
       Mass.: Harvard University Press (Harvard Studies in Compara-
       tive Literature, VI), 1921.
       Chapter VIII is entitled "Breton Lays" (pp. 199-226). Contains useful
       material on the translation of the *Lais* into Old Norse. See item 287.

287   —, 'The *Lais bretons* in Norway', in *Studies in Language and
       Literature in Honour of Margaret Schlauch.* Warsaw: P.W.N.,
       Polish Scientific Publishers, 1966, pp. 203-12.
       A shortened version of item 286.

288   Lefort de la Morinière, Adrien-Claude. *Bibliothèque poëtique,
       ou nouveau choix des plus belles pièces de vers en tout genre
       depuis Marot jusqu'aux poëtes de nos jours.* 4 vols, Paris,
       1745.
       The introduction, by Claude-Pierre Goujet, contains a reference (vol. I
       p. xlix) to Marie de France, taken almost textually from Guillaume
       Massieu, item 323.

289   Le Gentil, Pierre. 'A Propos du *Lai du Chèvrefeuille* et de
       l'interprétation des textes médiévaux', in *Mélanges offerts à
       Henri Chamard.* Paris: Nizet, 1951, pp. 17-27.
       The message contained in ll. 61-78 was, in Marie's mind, engraved on the
       bâton in addition to Tristan's name, perhaps in the form of a brief
       explanation followed by ll. 77-8. The written words take on their full
       meaning only in Iseut's 'âme complice'. No letter was sent by Tristan in
       advance. Such an interpretation fulfils the demands of both logic and
       poetry (cf. Spitzer, item 424).

290   Legge, J.G. *Chanticleer: A Study of the French Muse.*
       London: Dent, 1935.
       Contains some general remarks on Marie and a translation of ten lines of
       Chevrefoil (ll. 69-78), pp. 14-16.

291   Legge, M. Dominica. *Anglo-Norman in the Cloisters.* Edin-
       burgh: Edinburgh University Press, 1950.
       Contains several references to Marie and useful background information.
       The *Lais* are dated 'nearer 1180 than 1170'.

292   —, *Anglo-Norman Literature and its Background.* Oxford: Clarendon Press, 1963.

Contains numerous references to Marie. The *Lais* receive particular attention on pp. 72-3, the *Fables* on p. 107 (seen as 'aristocratic, but not courtly, literature'), and the *Espurgatoire* on pp. 204-5.

293   Lejeune, Rita. 'Rôle littéraire d'Aliénor d'Aquitaine et de sa famille', *Cultura Neolatina*, XIV (1954), 5-57.

Section 10 is entitled 'Aliénor et Marie de France'. The geography of the early *lais*, it is suggested, can be explained in terms of Eleanor's sojourns at Sherborne, Marlborough, Argentan, etc.

294   Levi, Ezio. 'Sulla cronologia delle opere di Maria di Francia', *Nuovi Studi Medievali*, I (1923), 41-72.

Proposes the chronology *Lais* (before 1183), *Espurgatoire* (about 1185), *Fables* (after 1189).

Reviews by:

.1   G. Bertoni, *Archivum Romanicum*, VII (1923), 401-6.

.2   L. Foulet, *Romania*, XLIX (1923), 131-4.

295   —, 'Una gemma della poesia medievale: il *lai* di *Eliduc'*, *Nuova Antologia di Lettere, Scienze ed Arti*, 6th series, CXCIII (Jan.-Feb., 1918), 64-80.

Contains a general introduction (pp. 63-4) and a prose translation of *Eliduc*, which must have been written by 1168 because of its influence on *Ille et Galeron*, and which is probably one of Marie's earliest *lais*.

296   —, 'I *lais* brettoni e la leggenda di Tristano', *Studi Romanzi*, XIV (1917), 113-246. Also in separate print, Perugia: Unione Tipografica Cooperativa, 1918.

A useful study. Contains a discussion of *Eliduc*, in which the hero is seen as a 'Tristano più umano' (p. 137), and of *Chevrefoil* (pp. 135-48). Also includes a section on the originality of Marie de France (pp. 236-40).

Reviews by:

.1   G. Bertoni, *Archivum Romanicum*, II (1918), 245-52.

.2   L. Foulet, *Romania*, XLVII (1921), 159-60.

.3   J.J. Salverda de Grave, *Neophilologus*, VIII (1923), 76-8.

297   —, 'Maria di Francia e le abbazie d'Inghilterra', *Archivum Romanicum*, V (1921), 472-93. Reprint: see 300.

Marie is identified with the Abbess of Reading principally on the basis of the role of convents in *Yonec*, *Le Fresne* and *Eliduc*. Still of interest.

Reviews by:

.1   L. Foulet, *Romania*, XLIX (1923), 131-4.

.2   A. Wallensköld, *Neuphilologische Mitteilungen*, XXIV (1923), 54-5.

298   —, 'Marie de France e il romanzo di *Eneas', Atti del Reale Istituto Veneto di Scienze, Lettere ed Arti,* LXXXI (1921-2), 645-86.

A well documented but unsuccessful attempt to prove that Marie is the author of the *Roman d'Eneas. Eliduc* in particular is seen as close in spirit and language: 'Tutto il romanzo di *Eneas* è pieno di spunti e di motivi del lai di *Eliduc'* (p. 671). See items 223, 397 and 398.
Review by:

.1   G. Bertoni, *Archivum Romanicum,* VII (1923), 401-6.

299   —, 'Il quinto *lai* di Maria di Francia: *Lanval', Nuova Antologia di Lettere, Scienze ed Arti,* 6th series, CXCIII (March-April, 1918), 51-62.

Contains a general introduction (pp. 51-3) and a prose translation of *Lanval.*

300   —, 'Il Re giovane e Maria di Francia', *Archivum Romanicum,* V (1921), 448-71. Reprint (with 297), Florence: Olschki, 1922.

Argues compellingly for the identification of the *nobles reis* with the young King Henry (Henri au Cort Mantel) and sees the *cunte Willame* of the *Fables* as William Marshal (1146-1219). The article contains interesting observations on the literary and political elements in Marie's poetry.

301   — , 'Troveri ed abbazie', *Archivio Storico Italiano,* LXXXIII (1925), 45-81. Also in separate print Florence: Olschki, 1925.

Discusses several issues relevant to Marie de France, e.g. the monastery at Reading and the identification of count William as William Marshal (pp. 48-50).
Reviews by:

.1   A. Hilka, *Zeitschrift für romanische Philologie,* XLVI (1926), 503-4.
.2   M. Roques, *Romania,* LIII (1927), 283-4.

302   Locke, F.W. 'A New Date for the Composition of the *Tractatus de purgatorio sancti Patricii', Speculum,* XL (1965), 641-6.

The *Tractatus,* which Marie definitely used, was in all probability dedicated to Henricus, seventh abbot of Warden. As Lawrence, the sixth abbot, was still alive in 1208 and Henricus left Warden on April 8th, 1215 (d. 1216), the *Tractatus* must have been composed during this seven-year period.

303   Lods, Jeanne. 'Quelques aspects de la vie quotidienne chez les conteurs du XIIe siècle', *Cahiers de Civilisation Médiévale,* IV

(1961), 23-45.
Contains details taken from the *Lais*.

304 —, 'Sur quelques vers de *Guigemar* (v. 145-150)', *Romania*, LXXVII (1956), 494-6.

L. 150 ('Braz fu de mer, hafne i aveit') should not be seen as a self-contained unit, but in conjunction with l. 149 ('De une ewe ke desuz cureit'). What Guigemar sees is a transformation in the landscape normally familiar to him. The ewe, 'stream', has become an arm of the sea, with a harbour. Some changes in punctuation are thus necessary at the end of ll. 147 and 148.

305 —, 'Marie de France', in *Dictionnaire des lettres françaises: Le MoyenAge, edited* by R. Bossuat, L. Pichard and G. Raynaud de Lage. Paris: Fayard, 1964.

306 Lot, Ferdinand. 'Etudes sur la provenance du cycle arthurien: I. Le sens du mot *breton* au XIIe siècle; II. De la provenance des lais dits bretons', *Romania*, XXIV (1895), 497-528.

Studies the terms *breton* and *Bretagne* in the *Lais* (pp. 514-28).
Review by:

.1 J. Loth, *Annales de Bretagne*, XI (1895), 478-81.

307 —, 'La Patrie des lais bretons', *Romania*, XXVIII (1899), 1-48.

A reply to Brugger's article, item 107. Marie's place names are discussed on pp. 25-48, in particular Carwent, Carlion and Carduel.

308 Lot-Borodine, Myrrha. *De l'amour profane à l'amour sacré: études de psychologie sentimentale au moyen âge.* Paris: Nizet, 1961.

Marie is discussed on pp. 31-5. General remarks, well expressed but superficial.

309 Loth, J. '*Le Lai du Bisclavret*: le sens de ce nom et son importance', *Revue Celtique*, XLIV (1927), 300-7.

Clothes act, like the magic ring in the *lai* of *Melion*, as an agent of transformation. The term *bisclavret* is related to *bisc*, 'short' and *lavret*, 'wearing breeches or short trousers'. The Bisclavret would thus be 'le court, l'insuffisamment, le mal vêtu'. Some detail concerning the clothing, contained in the primitive legend, has not been transmitted.

310 — , 'Des nouvelles théories sur l'origine des romans arthuriens', *Revue Celtique*, XIII (1892), 475-503.

Useful background material. The names Guigemar, Lanval and others are discussed on p. 481.

311   Lyons, Faith. 'The Bird as Messenger of Love in XIIth-century Courtly Literature', *Bibliographical Bulletin of the International Arthurian Society,* XXI (1969), 158.
Summary of a paper delivered at the IXth International Arthurian Congress, Cardiff 1969. Contains references to *Yonec, Laüstic* and *Milun.*

312   —, 'Marie de France, Ducis et les *Deux Amants*: légende locale et genèse poétique', *Bibliographical Bulletin of the International Arthurian Society,* XIX (1967), 119-27. Summary *ibid.,* XVIII (1966), 163.
Remarks on the revival of the legend of the Two Lovers in the eighteenth and nineteenth centuries, in particular in the poem of Ducis, published in 1813.

313   McKeehan, Irene P. *'Guillaume de Palerne*: a Medieval "Best Seller" ', *Publications of the Modern Language Association of America,* XLI (1926), 785-809.
Guillaume de Palerne is compared in some detail to *Bisclavret, Melion* and other werewolf stories.

314   Maillard, Jean. *Evolution et esthétique du lai lyrique des origines à la fin du XIVe siècle.* Paris: C.D.U., 1963.
A wide-ranging study with particular emphasis on the musical element in the *lai.* Contains a good bibliography (pp. viii-xii), an inventory of *lais* (pp. 98-106) and sections dealing with the term *lai* (pp. 1-11), the theory of origins (pp. 24-32) and the Breton lay (pp. 36-65).

315   —, 'Le Lai et la note du *Chèvrefeuille',* *Musica Disciplina,* XIII (1959), 3-13.
Offers a musical transcription of the *Lai du Chèvrefeuille,* possibly the one composed by Tristan.

316   Mall, Eduard, *De aetate rebusque Mariae Francicae nova quaestio instituitur.* Halle, 1867, 59pp.
A general study of biographical details concerning Marie and of her language. Concludes unacceptably that Marie was born and raised in Compiègne, spent a great part of her life in England and flourished around the middle of the thirteenth century. The *Lais* were dedicated to Henry III and composed around 1245, the *Fables* were for Guillaume de Dampierre, count of Flanders, and written about 1248. The *Espurgatoire* seems to have been written after 1250.

317   —, 'Zur Geschichte der Legende vom Purgatorium des heil. Patricius', *Romanische Forschungen,* VI (1891), 139-97.
Presents two Latin texts of the legend of St Patrick's Purgatory,

designated as the Bamberg and Colgan texts. Neither was the direct source of Marie's version.

318   — , 'Zur Geschichte der mittelalterlichen Fabellitteratur und insbesondere des *Esope* der Marie de France', *Zeitschrift für romanische Philologie,* IX (1885), 161-203.
A complex and detailed study. Concludes that Marie faithfully translated a collection of fables in English, composed at the beginning of the twelfth century or a little later. The first part of the English text is a free rendering of the *Romulus Nilanti,* the second the work of the English author himself. See item 454.

319   — , Noch einmal: Marie de Compiègne und das *Evangile aux femmes', Zeitschrift für romanische Philologie,* I (1877), 337-56.
Marie de France is definitely not the author of the *Evangile aux femmes.* See item 130.

320   Maraud, André. 'Le Lai de *Lanval* et la *Chastelaine de Vergi:* la structure narrative', *Romania,* XCIII (1972), 433-59.
A detailed and useful analysis of the two texts. Eight common narrative elements are identified, but in overall structure and in the significance of the common factors the texts display marked differences.

321   Marchiori, Marina. 'Note sul *Lanval* e la retorica medioevale', *Giornale Italiano di Filologia,* new series, II (1971), 186-93.
Sees Marie's poetry as strongly influenced by rhetorical tradition. Superficial study.

322   Martineau-Génieys, Christine. 'Du *Chievrefoil,* encore et toujours', *Le Moyen Age,* LXXVIII (1972), 91-114.
An interpretation stressing the poetic quality of the text with frequent references to more modern texts, in particular the *Princesse de Clèves.* The honeysuckle represents Yseut, the hazel Tristan. Trees are essentially male symbols. The *bastun* bore only Tristan's name in letters written vertically. From this sign Yseut reconstitutes the message which forms the heart of the *lai* in accordance with the laws of 'psychologie amoureuse'. The article concludes with some remarks on the poetic structure of *Chevrefoil.*
Review by:
.1   G. Di Stefano, *Studi Francesi,* XLIX (1973), 110.

323   Massieu, Guillaume. *Histoire de la poësie françoise; avec une défense de la poësie.* Paris, 1739.
Contains an early reference to Marie de France as translator of the Fables of Aesop (pp. 157-8). See Baum, item 85, p. 63.

324   Matzke, John E. 'The Lay of *Eliduc* and the Legend of the Husband with Two Wives', *Modern Philology*, V (1907-8), 211-39.

Broadens the scope of the discussion of G. Paris (item 350). The lay of *Eliduc* is seen as a combination of two elements, the exile and return motif (as found in *Horn et Rimenhild, Ille et Galeron* and *Mainet),* and the resemblance theme, in which due to the deceptive similarity of two persons of the same sex, confusion is occasioned with a member of the opposite sex (as in *Amis et Amiles, Le Fresne,* etc.). A detailed and useful study. See the remarks of W.A. Trindade, item 443.

325   — , 'The Source and Composition of *Ille et Galeron*', *Modern Philology*, IV (1906-7), 471-88.

Concerns the relationship of *Ille* to *Eliduc.*

326   Meissner, Rudolf. *Die Strengleikar: ein Beitrag zur Geschichte der altnordischen Prosalitteratur.* Halle: Niemeyer, 1902, ix + 320pp.

Contains a detailed comparison of Marie's text with the Old Norse version of her *Lais* (esp. pp. 258-92). Includes some influential comments on the text of the *Lais,* in particular on the Prologue (pp. 280-3). See items 147, 263 and 416.

327   Ménard, Philippe. 'La Déclaration amoureuse dans la littérature arthurienne au XIIe siècle', *Cahiers de Civilisation Médiévale,* XIII (1970), 33-42.

Contains a section entitled 'La diversité des aveux dans les *Lais* de Marie de France' (pp. 35-8). Six male and five female declarations are encountered. Arguments are short and responses not normally dictated by moral scruples. Women, however, hesitate to make the first move and often use messengers to veil their proposal. Sexual relations often follow promptly upon the declaration.
Summary in *Bibliographical Bulletin of the International Arthurian Society,* XXI (1969), 151-2.

328   — , *Le Rire et le sourire dans le roman courtois en France au moyen âge (1150-1250).* Geneva: Droz (Publications Romanes et Françaises, CV), 1969.

Contains numerous references to Marie's *Lais.*

329   Méon, D.M. *Le Roman du Renart.* 4 vols, Paris, 1826.

The *Couronnement de Renard* is attributed to Marie (vol. I, p. vii). The count to whom Marie dedicated the *Fables* is Guillaume de Dampierre, count of Flanders. Marie herself must have been Flemish.

330 Mermier, Guy R. 'En relisant le *Chevrefoil* de Marie de France', *French Review,* XLVIII (1974-5), 864-70.

Supports Delbouille's view (item 146), that Tristan sent a message to Iseut on a previous occasion. This message could have been a letter, perhaps wrapped round a hazel branch or written in ogamic script, but it is more likely to have been just a hazel branch, possibly with the encircling tentacles of the honeysuckle. Marie reports the message, translating Yseut's understanding of Tristan's signal.

331 Mickel, Emanuel J., Jr. *Marie de France.* New York: Twayne (Twayne's World Authors Series, CCCVI), 1974, 189pp.

A sound and readable general study. Chapter headings are: (1) Texts and Identity of Marie de France; (2) Intellectual Background of the Twelfth Century; (3) *Fables*; (4) *Espurgatoire Seint Patriz*; (5) The Narrative *lai*; (6) Plots and Sources; (7) Marie's Concept of Love; (8) Narrative Aspects of the *Lais.* Good bibliography and index.

332 — , 'Marie de France's Use of Irony as a Stylistic and Narrative Device', *Studies in Philology,* LXXI (1974), 265-90. Also appeared in *Cultura Neolatina,* XXXIII (1973), 33-53.

A wide-ranging study of irony, which is seen as illuminating characters and their relationship to the action and also casting light on Marie's own attitude towards her subject. Loyal, unselfish love helps characters to escape from the irony inherent in life.

333 — , 'A Reconsideration of the *Lais* of Marie de France', *Speculum,* XLVI (1971), 39-65.

A subtle analysis of the theme of love in the *Lais,* with particular stress on the nature or quality of love. For example, the love in *Equitan* is concupiscence, in *Le Fresne* a love of charity, and in *Guigemar* a *passio* which is later ennobled by the loyalty of the contemporary religious and secular commentaries, e.g., the fourteenth-century commentary on the poem *Les Echecs amoureux.* In *Eliduc* a relationship is developed between human love and divine love. The *parfit'amur* enjoyed by the couple (l. 1150) is love of a human being without ulterior motive, and such love has its natural source and goal in God.
Review by:
.1 F. Beggiato, *Cultura Neolatina,* XXXII (1972), 312-13.

334 — , 'The Unity and Significance of Marie's Prologue', *Romania,* XCVI (1975), 83-91.

The Prologue is seen as presenting two prominent theses: a) one has an obligation to use God-given talents; b) the ancients wrote obscurely so that later scholars could undertake a serious study of the texts. The first thesis appears in ll. 1-4 and is developed in ll. 5-8. The second is stated in ll. 9-16 and amplified in ll. 17-27. The expression *grevos' ovre* (25) is the key which links these two major elements. The author takes issue with earlier interpreters of the Prologue on a number of points, in particular l. 19 ('Cum plus trespasserunt le tens'), which is rendered plausibly as 'the more they (future commentators) will spend time'. See item 239.

335   Murrell, E.S. *'Chievrefueil* and Thomas' *Tristan', Arthuriana*, I (1929), 58-62.

Argues that Thomas' *Tristan* is the source of Marie's lay. No convincing evidence.

336   Nagel, E. 'Marie de France als dichterische Persönlichkeit', *Romanische Forschungen*, XLIV (1930), 1-102.

A wide-ranging study embracing almost all the preoccupations of other scholars and containing sections on Marie's life and works, chronology, the theme of love, the *merveilleux* and the religious life in the *Lais*, the sources of the *Espurgatoire* and the *Fables*, Marie's style, the characteristics of her heroes and heroines, etc. Abundant references to all the *Lais.*

337   Nagel, Rolf. 'A propos de *Fresne* (v. 261-272)', *Cahiers de Civilisation Médiévale*, X (1967), 455-6.

The term *fraternité* in l. 267 is a technical legal term corresponding to *fraternitas, familiaritas*, etc. In order to gain access to Fresne, Gurun gives the convent a gift of land (263-4), thus gaining the right of *retur, repaire* and *sejur* (265-6) granted to a benefactor.

338   Neri, Ferdinando. 'Appunti su *Guigemar', Annali dell'Istituto Superiore di Magistero di Torino*, VII (1933), 151-60.

Indicates some interesting parallels between *Guigemar* and the legend of Prodesaggio. See P. Rajna, *Dalla storia di Messere Prodesaggio*, Florence, 1916. See also item 10.

339   Newstead, Helaine. 'The Traditional Background of *Partonopeus de Blois', Publications of the Modern Language Association of America*, LXI (1946), 916-46.

Lanval is discussed as a close analogue of the fairy mistress theme of *Partonopeus.* Reference also to the boat motif in *Guigemar,* (pp. 930-1).

340   Nolting-Hauff, Ilse. 'Symbol und Selbstdeutung: Formen der erzählerischen Pointierung bei Marie de France', *Archiv für das Studium der neueren Sprachen und Literaturen*, CXCIX (1963), 26-33.

Analyses *Laüstic, Chevrefoil* and *Chaitivel.* The concentration of symbols in these *lais* gives them their profound meaning and makes them excellent examples of the genre.

341 Noomen, Willem. 'Le Lai des *Deus Amanz* de Marie de France: Contribution pour une description', in *Etudes de langue et de littérature du moyen âge offertes à Félix Lecoy.* Paris: Champion, 1973, pp. 469-81.

The author offers a 'description intégrale et explicite' of the text of the *Deus Amanz,* based on the method and terminology of Roman Jakobson and Claude Bremond. The perspectives of the three main characters, the king, the young lover and the daughter are analysed in turn with the aim of following the train of events measured in accordance with the 'échelle des possibilités logiques'. The subject matter of the text is three human destinies and none of the ambitions formulated is realized. The lover's death thwarts the father's plans and puts an end to his own objective which he shared with the king's daughter. In spite of the subtlety of the analysis and the fruitful nature of the method used, the fault committed by the young man, seen as 'une tentative irrationnelle d'auto-destruction', remains inadequately explained.

342 Nutt, A. 'The *lai* of *Eliduc* and the *Märchen* of Little Snow-White', *Folklore,* III (1892), 26-48.

Eliduc must owe its origin to a tale akin to the Gaelic legend of Gold-tree and Silver-tree, which represents a story flourishing in the tenth century and which may have given rise to the Southern Italian and North German Little Snow White tales.

343 Oesterley, Hermann. *Romulus: die Paraphrasen des Phaedrus und die Aesopische Fabel im Mittelalter.* Berlin, 1870.

The relationship between Marie's collection and the Latin fables presented here is discussed on pp. xxv-xxxvii.

344 Ogle, M.B. 'Some Theories of Irish Literary Influence and the Lay of *Yonec'*, *Romanic Review,* X (1919), 123-48.

Scholars who consider that the primary source of early French poems is Irish legend tend to pay little attention to their oriental and classical sources. *Yonec* contains at least nine elements which are not Celtic. This suggests that twelfth-century French writers had access to a large number of non-Celtic tales. See items 138, 241 and 253.

345 — , 'The Stag-Messenger Episode', *American Journal of Philology,* XXXVII (1916), 387-416.

The hind episode in *Guigemar* is discussed on pp. 391-3. The real messenger is not the hind, as is normally stated, but the stag. The hind and her fawn are allegorical representations of the lady and her niece.

346 O'Sharkey, Eithne M. 'The Identity of the Fairy Mistress in

Marie de France's *Lai de Lanval'*, *Trivium*, VI (1971), 17-25.
Lanval's mistress, a person of great wealth and authority, Queen of the supernatural land of Avalon, is probably to be identified with Morgain. Her relationship with Lanval is typical both of that between a Celtic fairy and the chosen hero and between a courtly lady and an Arthurian knight, and she must be considered as Marie's ideal heroine. This *lai* also provides the earliest example of the theme of enmity between Morgain and Guinevere and between Morgain and Arthur.
Summary in *Bibliographical Bulletin of the International Arthurian Society*, XXI (1969), 146-7.

347   Owen, D.D.R. *The Vision of Hell: Infernal Journeys in Medieval French Literature*. Edinburgh & London: Scottish Academic Press, 1970.
Contains some remarks on Marie's *Espurgatoire*, pp. 64-6. Marie intended her work for a wider public than the nobility. She was attracted to Henry of Saltrey's *Tractatus* both for its 'salutary moral tone' and for its 'value as an adventure story'.

348   Painter, Sidney. 'To Whom were Dedicated the *Fables* of Marie de France?' *Modern Language Notes*, XLVIII (1933), 367-69. Reprinted in *Feudalism and Liberty*. Baltimore: Johns Hopkins Press, 1961, pp. 107-10.
Identification of Marie's *Cunte Willalme* with William de Mandeville, earl of Essex, who became earl in 1167 and died in 1189.

349   Paris, Gaston. 'Lais inédits de *Tyolet*, de *Guingamor*, de *Doon*, du *Lecheor* et de *Tydorel'*, *Romania*, VIII (1879), 29-72.
Lays printed from MS Bibliothèque Nationale, Nouv. Acq. fr. 1104. The introduction contains interesting remarks on the provenance of Marie's *Lais*, on the geography of the *Lais* and on the terms *breton, Bretagne*, etc. (pp. 33-9). The *lais* published here, with the exception of the *Lecheor*, may, Paris says, be by Marie, but she is not a thirteenth-century author. Count William is not Guillaume de Dampierre. The *nobles reis* is probably Henry II.
Review by:
.1   E. Mall, *Zeitschrift für romanische Philologie*, III (1879), 298-304.

350   —, 'La Légende du mari aux deux femmes', *Revue Bleue*, 3rd series, XIV (July-Dec. 1887), 651-6. Reprinted in *La Poésie au moyen âge: leçons et lectures*. 2nd series, Paris: Hachette, 1895, pp. 109-30.
Situates *Eliduc* in the context of other legends dealing with a similar theme. See items 82, 324 and 443.

351 —, *La Littérature française au moyen âge (xi-xive siècle).* 5th ed. Paris: Hachette, 1914.

The Breton lays are the subject of pp. 97-9. Suggests the probable attribution to Marie of the *Lai de l'Espine, Tydorel* and *Guingamor.*

352 —, *Mélanges de littérature française du moyen âge,* ed. Mario Roques. Paris: Champion, 1912. Reprint, New York: Burt. Franklin, 1971, vii-i + 710pp.

Contains a number of isolated comments of interest. Marie did not know Breton (p. 43). The English titles which she gives to two of the lays indicates that their themes were also known in an English form (p. 44). The Breton lay must have belonged to diverse Celtic peoples and been current in both England and France (p. 44). *Ille et Galeron* was borrowed not from *Eliduc,* but from a lay with certain features resembling those in Marie's lay (p. 47). The reference to the form *garwulf* in *Bisclavret* indicates a Norman source for this lay (p. 79). Marie is probably the author of the *Lai de l'Espine* (p. 623).

353 —, 'Romans en vers du cycle de la Table Ronde', in *Histoire littéraire de la France,* XXX (1888), pp. 1-270.

The *Lais* are discussed on pp. 7-9. A British provenance is suggested for at least some of the Old French *lais,* in accordance with the general conclusion that 'La *matière de Bretagne* nous vient surtout d'Angleterre' (p. 3).

Review by:

.1 H. Zimmer (item 481).

354 Pasquier, Etienne. *Les Recherches de la France, augmentees en ceste derniere edition de trois livres entiers, outre plusieurs chapitres entrelassez en chacun des autres livres, tirez de la bibliotheque de l'Autheur.* Paris, 1621.

Refers to a *damoiselle* translator of fables (book VIII, chapter I, pp. 674-5), with a quotation from the Epilogue to Marie's *Fables.*

355 Paton, Lucy A. *Studies in the Fairy Mythology of Arthurian Romance.* Boston: Radcliffe College Monographs, XIII, 1903; 2nd ed. New York: Franklin (Burt Franklin Bibliographical Series, XVIII), 1960.

Chapter V ('Morgain and Guiomar') contains some useful remarks on *Guigemar* (pp. 65ff.).

356 Payen, Jean-Charles, *Le Lai narratif.* Turnhout: Brepols (*Typologie des sources du moyen âge occidental,* fasc. XIII, pp. 33-63), 1975.

Excellent general survey. Chapter headings are (1) Définition; (2) Evolution du genre; (3) Structure du lai; (4) Le public du lai; (5) Le rayonnement des lais; (6) L'établissement des textes; (7) L'intérêt historique. Good bibliography.

357   —, *Littérature française. Le moyen âge. I. Des origines à 1300.* Paris: Arthaud, 1970.
The section on the *Lais* (pp. 152-5) contains some penetrating observations.

358   —, *Le Motif du repentir dans la littérature française médiévale (des origines à 1230).* Geneva: Droz (Publications Romanes et Françaises, XCVIII), 1967.
Chapter IV is entitled 'Le lai narratif'. Particular attention is devoted to *Lanval* (pp. 308-12), *Eliduc* and *Equitan* (pp. 312-20) and *Guigemar* (pp. 325-8). Pp. 320-5 deal with 'la démesure dans le lai'. Many useful remarks.

359   —, 'Structure et sens d'*Yonec*', *Le Moyen Age,* LXXXII (1976), 263-87.
The text of *Yonec* is analysed by means of 'lectures successives' entitled (I) 'Séquences narratives et programmations' (presents the elements of the plot and points to a 'structure circulaire'), (II) 'L'espace et le temps' (the circular structure depends on three distinct temporalities, that of the *conte,* that of the *lai* and that of the legend), (III) 'Thèmes, contexte et modèles (eight themes, the *maumariée,* the imprisonment, the bird-lover, the transformation in the lady through love, the trap, the impossible jump, the journey to the other world and the vengeance, are placed in their context and provided with analogous contemporary models), (IV) 'Sens d'*Yonec*' (the text has more than one meaning and stresses that the world is wicked, that love is justified by its intensity, that the right to happiness is imprescriptible). Above all *Yonec* illustrates Marie's pleasure in telling a story and in its technique it resembles that used in the cinema.

360   Pelan, Margaret. *L'Influence du Brut de Wace sur les romanciers français de son temps.* Paris: Droz, 1931.
The influence of Wace on Marie is discussed on pp. 104-24. She found in the *Brut* not only a framework for her *Lais,* but also descriptions of people and things, certain narrative features and stylistic devices.

361   Philipot, E. and J. Loth. 'Le Lai du *Lecheor* et *Gumbelauc*', *Revue Celtique,* XXVIII (1907), 327-36.
Contains some interesting remarks on *Chaitivel* with which the *Lai du Lecheor* can be compared. The standard view of the content of a lay is often too narrow. There is no need for an element of mystery or magic.

362   Pickens, Rupert T. *'Equitan:* Anti-*Guigemar', Romance Notes,* XV (1973-4), 361-7.

Guigemar and *Equitan* set the tone of the whole collection of *lais* by presenting the contrasting destinies of their heroes, who love ladies of different characters and are induced by love to commit acts of an anti-social nature. All consuming passion can lead in two directions, to redemption (*Guigemar*) and to ignoble defeat (*Equitan*). Love is an amoral force, rendered good or bad by the hero's ultimate fate, happiness or disaster.

363   —, 'Thematic Structure in Marie de France's *Guigemar', Romania,* XCV (1974), 328-41.

Lines 57-8 of *Guigemar* ('De tant i out mespris nature / Kë unc de nul' amur n'out cure') must be understood as 'To such an extent had nature wronged him that never did he care for any kind of love'. Nature is thus the cause of Guigemar's sexual problem with its adverse social consequences. Guigemar moves through a number of stages to a consciousness of his identity as a man and to harmony in his personal and social life. His destiny is controlled by God, who dominates the hierarchy God, Nature, Love. The androgynous hind, acting as a messenger of God and representing sexual wholeness or the perfect union of man and woman, is the intermediary between the closed world of Brittany, in which Guigemar cannot function, and the *antive cité,* his personal world, an 'Avalon-like, often irrational other world'. On his return to Brittany Guigemar is again unmindful of his social obligation to take a wife. His *destinee* (108) is finally accomplished after he has won his lady by the exercise of prowess at the castle of Meriadu , a violent man smitten by lust for the lady. *Guigemar* can be said to illustrate the role of love and sexuality both in individual lives and in the universal creative scheme.

364   Piramus, Denis. *La Vie Seint Edmund le Rei, poème anglo-normand du XIIe siècle,* ed. H. Kjellman, Gothenburg, 1935.

The following lines seem to refer to Marie de France: 'E dame Marie autresi, Ki en rime fist e basti E compassa les vers de lais, Ke ne sunt pas tel tut verais; E si en est ele mult loée E la rime par tutu amée, Kar mult l'aiment, si l'unt cher Cunte, barun e chivaler; E si enaiment mult l'escrit E lire le funt, si unt delit, E si les funt sovent retreire. Les lais solent as dames pleire, De joie les oient e de gré, Qu'il sunt sulum lur volenté' (35-48).

365   Pollmann, Leo. *Die Liebe in der hochmittelalterlichen Literatur Frankreichs: Versuch einer historischen Phänomenologie.* Frankfurt: Klostermann (Analecta Romanica, XVIII), 1966.

Contains a chapter entitled *'Fin'amor* in den *Lais* der Marie de France' (pp. 309-19). Deals principally with *Equitan, Chaitivel* and *Guigemar.*

366   Potter, Murray A. *Sohrab and Rustem: the Epic Theme of a Combat between Father and Son; a Study of its Genesis and Use in Literature and Popular Tradition.* London: Nutt, 1902.
Useful background for *Milun,* which is discussed on pp. 47-8.

367   Pratt, Robert A. 'Three Old French Sources of the *Nonnes Preestes Tale', Speculum,* XLVII (1972), 422-44, 646-68.
Marie's fable of the cock and the fox (ed. Warnke, no. LX) is seen as the main source of the fable section of the *Nonnes Preestes Tale.*

368   Prettyman, C.W. 'Peter von Staufenberg and Marie de France', *Modern Language Notes,* XXI (1906), 205-8.
Suggested parallels between *Lanval* and the Middle High German poem concerning Peter von Staufenberg.

369   Rajna, P. 'Le origini della novella narrata dal Frankeleyn nei *Canterbury Tales* del Chaucer', *Romania,* XXXII (1903), 204-67.
Pp. 224-34 deal with the relationship between Chaucer and the *Lais* of Marie.

370   Ranke, Friedrich. *Tristan und Isold.* Munich: Bruckmann, 1925.
Pp. 97-101 deal with *Chevrefoil,* offering principally a translation into German.

371   Reaney, Gilbert. 'Concerning the Origins of the Medieval *Lai', Music and Letters,* XXXIX (1958), 38-51.
The Breton *lais* were derived not as Wolf thought (item 476) from the Latin sequence, but from an old tradition of minstrelsy in which persistent rhythm, such as is found in the *chanson de geste,* was allied to variety of structure.

372   Reiffenberg, Le Baron de. *Chronique rimée de Philippe Mouskès.* 2 vols, Brussels: Hayez, 1836-8.
Marie is discussed on pp. cxciii-cxcix. The count referred to in the *Fables* must be French and was probably Guillaume de Dampierre (died 1251), son of Marguerite de Flandre (not her husband, as Legrand d'Aussy thought, item 56).

373   Reinhard, John R. *The Survival of Geis in Mediaeval Romance.* Halle: Niemeyer, 1933.
Comments on *Guigemar* (pp. 329-30) and on *Lanval* (pp. 240ff).

374   Reinhard, John R. and Vernam E. Hull. 'Bran and Sceolang', *Speculum*, XI (1936), 42-58.
Contains some useful remarks on werewolves (pp. 52ff.).

375   Renzi, Lorenzo. 'Recenti studi sui *lais* narrativi e su Marie de France', *Studi di Letteratura Francese*, I (1967), 117-26.
Discusses principally the studies by H. Baader (item 78) and J.A. Frey (item 193).

376   —, *Tradizione cortese e realismo in Gautier d'Arras*. Florence: Olschki (Università di Padova, Pubblicazioni della Facoltà di Lettere e Filosofia, XLII), 1964.
Contains abundant brief references to Marie, in particular to the relationship between *Eliduc* and *Ille et Galeron*.

377   Ribard, Jacques. 'Essai sur la structure du lai du *Chèvrefeuille*', in *Mélanges de langue et de littérature médiévales offerts à Pierre Le Gentil*. Paris: SEDES, 1973, pp. 721-4.
A short but useful analysis. The orchestration of the theme of unnatural separation in ll. 47-78 is an 'envolée lyrique' framed by a dry, realistic presentation of the same theme. The meeting in the forest, home of brigands, hermits and lovers, is prepared in concrete, precise terms and presented without symbols or poetry. Yseut's historical role as queen contrasts markedly with her role as 'bele amie'.

378   —, 'Le Lai du *Laostic:* structure et signification', *Le Moyen Age*, LXXVI (1970), 263-74.
A study of the structure and texture of the *lai*. Symbols other than the nightingale are stressed, the *fenestre* (40, 55, 73, 128), the *laçuns* (96, 124), the *glu* (99), etc. Opposition between two worlds is rightly underlined, between the window leading to another, more open, universe, and the mediocrity of the present world. The nightingale symbolizes the impossibility of any communication between these two worlds. Structurally the text can be divided into three tableaux, 7-56 (the exposition), 57-120 (the action), and 121-156 (the 'apaisement progressif'). Line 120 ('De la chambre s'en ist atant ') marks a complete break in the poem's movement.
Summary in *Bibliographical Bulletin of the International Arthurian Society*, XXI (1969), 147.
Review by:
.1   G. Di Stefano, *Studi Francesi*, XLIV (1971), 321-2.

379   Ringger, Kurt. 'Die altfranzösischen Verspurgatorien', *Zeitschrift für romanische Philologie*, LXXXVIII (1972), 389-402.

Marie's *Espurgatoire* is discussed in the context of other versions of the story. The legend of St Patrick's purgatory has become in Marie's version a courtly *aventure,* which suggests that its author is to be identified with the Marie who composed the *Lais.*

380 —, *Die Lais: zur Struktur der dichterischen Einbildungskraft der Marie de France.* Tübingen: Niemeyer (Beihefte zur *Zeitschrift für romanische Philologie,* CXXXVII), 1973, 174pp.

Contains three principal chapters, (1) Marie de France als historische Persönlichkeit, (2) Marie de France als literarhistorische Persönlichkeit, (3) Marie de France als poetische Persönlichkeit–Die *Lais.*

A dense study of considerable importance. Most of the historical and interpretative questions raised by Marie's works are discussed in detail. In particular chapter III (pp. 65-151) offers an important literary analysis of the *Lais,* which are seen as functioning according to three principles, a basic motif (love),a central concept (*aventure,* normally linked to magic) and a network of signs.

Reviews by:

.1   R. Dubuis, *Studi Francesi,* LVI (1975), 325.
.2   E.A. Francis, *Medium Aevum,* XLIV (1975), 296
.3   P. Jonin, *Cahiers de Civilisation Médiévale,* XVIII (1975), 170-3.
.4   E.J. Mickel, Jr., *Speculum,* LI (1976), 532-5.
.5   M.J.J. Spoor, *Rapports,* XLIV (1974), 108-12.
.6   P. Vernay, *Studi Medievali,* 3rd series, XIV (1973), 1206-9.
.7   P. Zumthor, *Vox Romanica,* XXXIV (1975), 329-31.

381 — , 'Marie de France und kein Ende', *Zeitschrift für romanische Philologie,* LXXXVI (1970), 40-8.

An article based on the conclusions of R. Baum (item 85), to which the author is favourably disposed, though he wisely stresses the need for further documentation and for thorough analyses of texts.

Reviews by:

.1   G. Di Stefano, *Studi Francesi,* LI (1973), 520.
.2   F. Lecoy, *Romania,* XCIII (1972), 421.

382 — , 'Zum *Nobles Reis* bei Marie de France: eine Richtigstellung', *Zeitschrift für romanische Philologie,* LXXXIII (1967), 495-7.

The identification of the 'nobles reis' (*Lais,* Prologue, l. 43) with Henry II is by no means as clear as some scholars (e.g. Bédier, item 89, p. 839 and Bezzola, item 93, p. 305) would suggest.

Review by:

.1   N. Mann, *Studi Francesi,* XXXVII (1969), 115.

383 Riquer, Martín de. 'La *aventure,* el *lai* y el *conte* en María de Francia', *Filologia Romanza,* II (1955), 1-19.

A thorough analysis of the passages in the *Lais* containing the terms under discussion. The Bretons (in *Eliduc* the 'ancien Bretun', ll. 1181-4) composed *lais* to commemorate events to which Marie gives the name *aventure.* She does not consider herself as the author of *lais.* Between the *aventure* and the *lai* there lies the *cunte* and Marie's own compositions can legitimately be called *contes.* Her readers were fully aware of the musical character of the *lai.* In the case of *Milun, Chaitivel* and *Chevrefoil* Marie is recounting the circumstances which gave rise to the *lai.*

Reviews by:

.1 A. Goosse, *Les Lettres Romanes,* XI (1957), 317.

.2 A. Pézard, *Romania,* LXXVII (1956), 397.

384 Robert, A.C.M. *Fables inédites des XIIe, XIIIe et XIVe siècles, et Fables de La Fontaine.* 2 vols, Paris: Cabin, 1825.

Marie is discussed in vol. I, pp. clii-clix. Concludes that she was born in Normandy or Brittany, came to England as a young girl and dedicated her *Lais* to Stephen about 1141. The count to whom she refers in the Epilogue to the *Fables* is William of Ypres, who helped to place Stephen on the throne. The *Fables* were originally translated from the Latin by Henry I.

385 Robertson, D.W., Jr. 'Love Conventions in Marie's *Equitan',* *Romanic Review,* XLIV (1953), 241-5.

Equitan is seen as a reflection of contemporary clerical attitudes towards carnal love, as expressed, for example, in the *De spirituali amicitia* of Ailred of Rievaulx. Lecherous love is not the result of careful deliberation. Stimulated through the ears *(Equitan,* 38ff) and the eyes (49ff), it knows no discretion or moderation. Marie's condemnation of sensuality is, as Hoepffner pointed out (item 220, p. 301), the result of a moralizing, didactic intention on her part.

386 —, 'Marie de France, *Lais,* Prologue, 13-16', *Modern Language Notes,* LXIV (1949), 336-8.

An unconvincing attempt to clarify ll. 13-16 of the Prologue in terms of exegetical practice. The lines are rendered as: 'So that those who were to come after them and to learn them might gloss the letter or grammatical structure and from the apparent sense determine the doctrinal content'.

387 Robertson, Howard S. 'Love and the Other World in Marie de France's *Eliduc',* in *Essays in Honor of Louis Francis Solano.* Chapel Hill: University of North Carolina Press (University of North Carolina Studies in Romance Languages and Litera-

tures, XCII), 1970, pp. 167-76.

Eliduc's experiences in England, to which he goes as a result of an intolerable situation in his own land, resemble those of Guigemar, Lanval and the lady in *Yonec* in the Other World. The text contains seven divisions, ll. 1-88, 89-270, 271-549, 550-704, 705-952, 953-1144, 1145-84. Episode four (ll. 550-704), in which Eliduc realizes that it would be disastrous to unite the real world with his Other World, is crucial. *Eliduc* shows that the survival of true human love in a world of duty and responsibility is achieved only by means of an act of charity.

388   Rohlfs, Gerhard. *Vom Vulgärlatein zum altfranzösischen: Einführung in das Studium der Altfranzösischen Sprache.* 3rd ed., Tübingen: Niemeyer, 1968. English translation by V. Almazan and L. McCarthy, Detroit: Wayne State University Press, 1970.

Contains a study of the language of *Bisclavret* (German version pp. 96-213, English translation, pp. 72-169).

389   Rothe, L. A. *Les Romans du Renard examinés, analysés et comparés.* Paris: Techener, 1845.

Rejects the attribution to Marie of the *Couronnement de Renard* and identifies *cunte Willame* as William Longsword (pp. 326-58). The *Lais* are seen as addressed to Henry III of England.

390   Rothschild, Judith R. *Narrative Technique in the Lais of Marie de France: Themes and Variations.* Vol. I, Chapel Hill (University of North Carolina Studies in Romance Languages and Literatures, CXXXIX), 1974.

Contains extended and useful analyses of *Equitan, Le Fresne, Bisclavret, Les Deus Amanz, Yonec* and *Milun.* Abundant literary, structural and thematic comments. A second volume will treat the remaining six poems. See item 504.

391   — , 'A Rapprochement between *Bisclavret* and *Lanval'*, *Speculum*, XLVIII (1973), 78-88.

Based on the presence in the *Lais* of basic narrative motifs or analogues repeated as primary or secondary elements of individual plot structure. Both texts under discussion here contain a king and a significant relationship between the protagonist and the king. *Bisclavret* has little descriptive detail; *Lanval* is rich in descriptive passages, with a good deal of emphasis on financial details. In particular the author stresses here the treatment of legal procedures in the two *lais,* which both contain the important term *felonie* (*Bisclavret,* 246; *Lanval,* 439). The concept of *felonia* in English law is discussed, with the important changes which took place in criminal law during the second half of the twelfth century.

392   Roulleau, Gabriel. *Etude chronologique de quelques thèmes narratifs des romans courtois.* Paris: Champion, [circa 1967].
A thesis, presented circa 1914, and published posthumously. Remarks on Marie's use of animals, pp. 11-12, and on the magic ship in *Guigemar*, pp. 29-30.

393   Rowbotham, John F. *The Troubadours and Courts of Love.*
London: Swan Sonnenschein; New York: Macmillan, 1895.
Marie is the subject of pp. 192-5. A general introduction, often misleading.

394   Sabatier, Robert. *Histoire de la poésie française: la poésie du moyen âge.* Paris: Michel, 1975.
Marie's work is discussed on pp. 121-4.

395   St.Clair, Foster Y. 'Marie de France's *Lai des Douz Amanz*', *North Dakota Quarterly*, XXX (1962), 80-7.
A verse translation in octosyllabic couplets with the original text follows a perceptive introduction.

396   —, 'Some English Translations of Marie de France', *Proceedings of the Linguistic Circle of Manitoba and North Dakota,* II, no. 1 (1960), 6-7.
The translations discussed are those by O'Shaughnessy (item 62), Weston (item 70), Luquiens (item 58), Rickert (item 64) and Mason (item 59). The need for a new, reliable English translation is stressed.

397   Salverda de Grave, J.J. *Eneas: texte critique.* Halle: Niemeyer (Bibliotheca Normannica, IV), 1891.
The introduction contains a comparison between the language of *Eneas* and that of the *Lais*. Several parallel passages are quoted. Concludes that: 'Il y a entre les *Lais* et l'*Eneas* une telle ressemblance de formes et de style qu'on ne saurait nier qu'ils se soient connus' (pp. xxii-xxiv). Review by:

.1   G. Paris, *Romania,* XXI (1892), 281-94. Paris suggests that Marie is the author of *Eneas.* See items 223, 298 and 398.

398   —, 'Marie de France et *Eneas*', *Neophilologus,* X (1925), 56-9.
Opposes Levi's suggestion that Marie is the author of *Eneas* (see item 298).

399   Savage, Edward B. 'Marie de France's *Chevrefoil* as Drama and Image: a Study in Breton Oral Tradition', in *Cairo Studies in English.* Cairo, 1960, pp. 139-53.

A stimulating study of the symbolic possibilities of the hazel and the honeysuckle. Marie's translation of *chevrefoil* as 'gotelef', a term not attested in Middle English, suggests that she was aware of the association of the goat and the honeysuckle. The love extolled by this *lai* may have 'deep roots in erotic pagan cults which, in turn, took the goat as the center of their fertility rites'. See items 400 and 505.

400   —, *The Rose and the Vine: a Study of the Evolution of the Tristan and Isolt Tale in Drama.* Cairo: The American University at Cairo Press, 1961.
A published version of item 505 containing a revised and expanded version of item 399 (pp. 11-33).

401   Schiött, Emil. *L'Amour et les amoureux dans les Lais de Marie de France.* Lund, 1889, 66pp.
A brief but effective study of Marie's conception of love, the qualities of her heroes and heroines and the relationship between some of the principal characters.

402   Schober, Rita. 'Kompositionsfragen in den *Lais* der Marie de France', *Wissenschaftliche Zeitschrift der Humboldt-Universität zu Berlin,* IV (1954-5), 43-59. Reprinted with some changes in *Von der wirklichen Welt in der Dichtung: Aufsätze zur Theorie und Praxis des Realismus in der französischen Literatur.* Berlin and Weimar: Aufbau-Verlag, 1970, pp. 112-36 (notes and Appendix, pp. 383-97).
Marie's view of *aventure* contrasts with that found in the romances, because it is seen as an inner experience, not as a collection of outward acts. As a result the subject matter of the *lais* is human and general in character. Their plots and themes are unified and well-rounded. The structure of the *lais* is linked to Marie's view of *aventure* and love. She is concerned to show love both at its inception and in its continuation. Thus the *lais* have a twin structure (e.g., in *Eliduc* the first part is presented from Eliduc's point of view, the second from that of the two women). Important elements in the stories are often repeated and descriptions of characters, noteworthy for their combination of brevity and relevance, are essentially realistic. The article concludes with an appendix on the use of the word *aventure* in the *lais*.

403   Schoepperle, Gertrude. 'Chievrefoil', *Romania,* XXXVIII (1909), 196-218. Reprinted with slight changes in *Tristan and Isolt: a Study of the Sources of the Romance.* 2nd ed., New York: Burt Franklin, 1960, vol. I, pp. 138-47, vol. II, pp. 301-15.
The variants of the episode recounted in *Chevrefoil* fall into three

categories: (a) Iseut finds by chance a carved piece of bark requesting a meeting (*Chevrefoil*); (b) a previous communication gives Iseut the message which in (a) was entrusted to the bark and warns her to watch for a signal (Eilhart von Oberge, Heinrich von Freiberg); (c) the piece of bark or twig is replaced by a conventional signal (*Sir Tristrem,* the *Saga,* Ulrich von Türheim). *Chevrefoil* represents the oldest and simplest version of the episode, but for ll. 62 and 109 the readings of MS S are to be preferred, as H has rationalized the event. Several Celtic parallels to the hazel on the highroad and the *Chevrefoil* episode may be a survival of a specifically Irish practice. An important study.

404 Schofield, William H.'Chaucer's Franklin's Tale', *Publications of the Modern Language Association of America,* XVI (1901), 405-49.
The Franklin's Tale in its fundamental theme and in its details shows a great similarity to extant Breton lays.

405 —, 'The Lay of *Guingamor', Harvard Studies and Notes in Philology and Literature,* V (1896), 221-43.
Contains periodic references to *Lanval,* esp. p. 230.
Review by:
.1 G. Paris, *Romania,* XXVII (1898),323.

406 —, 'The Lays of *Graelent* and *Lanval,* and the Story of Wayland', *Publications of the Modern Language Association of America,* XV (1900), 121-80.
A detailed and useful examination of the relations between the different versions of the story found in *Graelent* and *Lanval.* The former should not be attributed to Marie, nor should it unreservedly be considered as older than *Lanval* (cf. Hertz, item 50, p. 324; G. Paris, item 353, p. 9). For example, the way in which the hero comes into contact with the fairy in *Lanval* is closer to the original than the equivalent scenes in *Graelent.* In general Marie made only rare additions to her stories: 'For originality in conception or combination we look in vain in her work' (p. 163).
Reviews by:
.1 G. Huet, *Le Moyen Age,* XV (1902), 44-6.
.2 G. Paris, *Romania,* XXIX (1900), 487.

407 Schürr, Friedrich. *Das altfranzösische Epos: zur Stilgeschichte und inneren Form der Gotik.* Munich: Hueber, 1926.
Contains a chapter on Marie's *Lais,* pp. 366-87.

408 —, 'Das Aufkommen der *matière de Bretagne* im Lichte der veränderten literarhistorischen Betrachtung', *Germanisch-*

romanische Monatsschrift, IX (1921), 96-108.
Contains remarks on the meaning of *breton* and *Bretagne,* on the term *lai* and on the provenance of Marie's *Lais.*

409 —, 'Komposition und Symbolik in den *Lais* der Marie de France', *Zeitschrift für romanische Philologie,* L (1930), 556-82. Reprinted in *Erlebnis, Sinnbild, Mythos: Wege der Sinndeutung romanischer Dichtung.* Berne and Munich: Francke, 1968, pp. 17-42.
A response to Spitzer's article (item 425). Denies that the symbolic objects in the *lais* are always incarnations of an intellectual problem and that the *lais* are problematic in the modern sense. In each *lai* there is a central event possessed of significance rather than constituting a problem. Each *lai* is analysed with stress on the role of fate, the psychological and emotional qualities of the *lais,* the use of indirect narrative techniques. Symbolism in the *lais* is seen as the outward expression of spiritual and psychological reality.

410 Schultz-Gora, O. 'Zum Text und den Anmerkungen der dritten Auflage der *Lais* der Marie de France (ed. K. Warnke 1925)', *Zeitschrift für romanische Philologie,* XLVI (1926), 314-25.
A review of item 17. Important textual comments.

411 Scudéry, Madeleine de. *Conversations nouvelles sur divers sujets.* Paris, 1684.
Contains an early reference to Marie de France in a passage which reads: 'Je ne m'arreste pas à vous dire que dés le temps de S. Loüis Guillaume de Lory eut de la reputation, & Jean de Meun sous Philippes le Bel; & que Marot ressuscita leurs Ouvrages sous François premier; qu'il y eut une Demoiselle en ces vieux temps-là, qui traduisit les Fables d'Esope, & que l'usage de la Poësie en ces mesmes siécles estoit entre les personnes de la plus haute qualité' (pp. 773-4). See Baum, item 85, pp. 62-3.

412 Segre, Cesare. 'Per l'edizione critica dei *lai* di Maria di Francia', *Cultura Neolatina,* XIX (1959), 215-37.
An important and detailed analysis of the manuscripts of the *Lais,* with particular reference to Rychner's edition of *Lanval* (item 14). Suggests the classification HC; P (Q) S.
Review by:
.1 R. De Cesare, *Studi Francesi,* XIV (1961), 321.

413 —, *'Lanval, Graelent, Guingamor',* in *Studi in onore di Angelo Monteverdi.* Modena: Società Tipografica Editrice

Modenese, 1959, vol II, pp. 756-70. Reprint, Modena: Soc. Tip. Ed. Modenese, 1957, 17pp.

A detailed analysis of the three texts under discussion. *Guingamor* and *Graelent* are seen as deriving from Marie's *Lais,* in particular from *Lanval.* The order of composition is envisaged as *Lanval, Graelent, Guingamor.* See items 115, 228, 243.

Reviews by:

.1 R. De Cesare, *Studi Francesi,* VI (1958), 469.

.2 J. Lods, *Romania,* LXXIX (1958), 131-5.

.3 E. von Richthofen, *Cahiers de Civilisation Médiévale,* III (1960), 370-1.

414   —, 'Piramo e Tisbe nei *Lai* di Maria di Francia', in *Studi in onore di Vittorio Lugli e Diego Valeri.* Venice: Pozza, 1961, vol. II, pp. 845-53.

Concerns borrowings from Ovid in *Deus Amanz* and *Laüstic.*

Reviews by:

.1 R. De Cesare, *Studi Francesi,* XVI (1962), 120.

.2 F. Lecoy, *Romania,* LXXXIV (1963), 288.

415   Shippey, Thomas A. 'Listening to the Nightingale', *Comparative Literature,* XXII (1970), 46-60.

A useful study of the meaning of the nightingale in a number of medieval texts. *Laüstic* is the object of an extended discussion (pp. 51-2). Traditionally the nightingale is linked to the brevity, ecstasy and fatality of love. By the time of Marie, listening to the nightingale 'implies a blend of joy and sorrow, a longing for the ideal and far-off, together with the knowledge that this will only vanish in the moment of its capture'.

416   Skårup, Povl. 'Les *Strengleikar* et les lais qu'ils traduisent', in *Les Relations littéraires franco-scandinaves au moyen âge.* Actes du Colloque de Liège (avril, 1972). Liège, 1975, pp. 97-115.

A study of the *Strengleikar* can assist the student of the anonymous French *lais* and the *Lais* of Marie in a number of ways (choice of base MS, dating of text, etc.). In particular an analysis of the manuscript tradition of the general Prologue and the prologue to *Guigemar* lends support to the argument of R. Baum (item 85) that Marie is not necessarily the author of the twelve *lais* of the Harley collection. See items 147, 263 and 326.

417   *Smirnov, A.A. '*Lais* Marie de France i problemy badania francuskiej literatury dworskiej klasycznego średniowiecza', in *Romanogiermanskaja filologija.* Leningrad, 1957, pp. 263-80. Translated in *Etudes sur l'histoire de la littérature euro-*

péenne occidentale. Moscow and Leningrad, 1965, pp. 88-114 (under the title 'Les *Lais* de Marie de France et les lais anonymes').

418   Smith, Kirby F. 'An Historical Study of the Werwolf in Literature', *Publications of the Modern Language Association of America,* IX (1894), 1-42.

Bisclavret is discussed on pp. 11-13. The fact that Marie takes the side of the wolf is exceptional. She considers him an innocent victim whose transformations are an unfortunate necessity imposed upon him by nature.

419   Smith, M. Ellwood. 'A Classification for Fables, Based on the Collection of Marie de France', *Modern Philology,* XV (1917-18), 477-89.

The core of the fable aims at fixing certain truths in the minds of its readers by allegorical representation. Three groups of fables can be distinguished, those in which the actors (with the setting) and the action are symbolic, those in which the action is typical or realistic whereas the actors and the setting are symbolic, and those in which the actors are typical but the action is symbolic. Justification for this grouping is sought by recourse to the *Fables* of Marie.

420   Smithers, G.V. 'Story-patterns in some Breton Lays', *Medium Aevum,* XXII (1953), 61-92.

Three closely related story-patterns recur (sometimes in modified or garbled form) in several Old French and Middle English works. Type I (*Lanval, Graelent, Guingamor,* etc.) contains eight elements, but concerns principally the love of a mortal in unhappy circumstances for a fairy. In Type II the supernatural being fathers a son and gives the mother prophetic instructions (*Tydorel, Desiré, Yonec,* etc.). The son in Type III brings his parents together after an armed combat with his father (*Milun, Doon,* etc.). Useful and well argued.

421   Söderhjelm, Werner. *La Nouvelle française au XVe siècle.* Paris: Champion, 1910. Reprint, Geneva: Slatkine, 1973.

General remarks on Marie, pp. 1-2.

422   Söll, Ludwig. 'Altfranzösisch *grave* 'Wald'? bei Marie de France', *Archiv für das Studium der neueren Sprachen und Literaturen,* CCI (1965), 193-6.

The term *grave,* which occurs six times in the *Fables* of Marie, is linked to the Middle English *grave.*

423   Spitzer, Leo. 'Zur Auffassung der Kunst des Arcipreste de

Hita', *Zeitschrift für romanische Philologie,* LIV (1934),, 237-70. Translated (as 'En torno al arte del Arcipreste de Hita') in *Lingüística e historia literaria.* 2nd ed. Madrid: Gredos (Biblioteca Románica Hispánica, Estudios y Ensayos, XIX), 1961, pp. 87-134.

Contains remarks on the Prologue to the *Lais* and related exegetical problems (pp. 238ff.; pp. 89-90, 98, 100 of translation).

424   —, 'La *Lettre sur la baguette de coudrier* dans le lai du *Chievrefueil',* Romania, LXIX (1946-7), 80-90. Reprinted in *Romanische Literaturstudien 1936-1956.*Tubingen: Niemeyer, 1959, pp. 15-25.

Foulet's suggestion (item 176) of a letter sent by Tristan in advance of his meeting with Iseut and Schoepperle's view (item 403) that Marie has transported into her *lai* an ancient Irish motif cannot be accepted. The *lai* should be considered in the light of the distinction between the *esprit* and the *lettre,* drawn from patristic exegesis. The *lettre* is Tristan's name and ll. 61-78 recount Iseut's interpretation of Tristan's message to her, an interpretation inspired by the miraculous power of love. The *paroles* commemorated by Tristan in his *lai* are Iseut's words during the meeting of the lovers (cf. 1. 96: 'E ele li dist sun pleisir'). In his conclusion the author claims that: 'Il faudrait voir désormais dans Marie de France, plutôt qu'un poète rationaliste et un folklorisant moderne, une *anima naturaliter christiana.'*

425   —, 'Marie de France — Dichterin von Problem-Märchen', *Zeitschrift für romanische Philologie,* L (1930), 29-67.

Article of considerable importance and influence. Each *lai* is constructed round an intellectual problem concerning some aspect of love: e.g., in *Guigemar* the love-union arises through suffering, yet this suffering is humanly necessary; in *Lanval* love imposes an obligation to be discreet, and this obligation must not be contravened whatever the circumstances. In nearly all the *lais* the problem is incarnated in a symbolic object such as the casket in *Laüstic* or the *bastun* in *Chevrefoil.* The marvellous atmosphere of the *lais,* their situation in time,. and the realism and generality of their subject matter are also discussed. The *lais* are seen as an act of remembering (whence their situation in remote time and the use of fairy-tale elements), in such a way that, memory being integral to the act of composition, the *lais* themselves symbolise 'the laying of the experiences of love in a casket of memory'.

426   —, 'The Prologue to the *Lais* of Marie de France and Medieval Poetics', *Modern Philology,* XLI (1943-4), 96-102. Reprinted in *Romanische Literaturstudien 1936-1956.* Tübingen:

Niemeyer, 1959, pp. 8-14.

An influential but not closely argued study. Marie and other contemporary writers thought that their books would be glossed in accordance with the principles of Biblical exegesis. The *sen* in l. 16 of the
Prologue is seen as the 'Christian attitude (the *intelletto sano* of Dante)
in which the interpreters consult the pagan authors, whose *purpose* it
was... to veil, with the obscurity of poetic form, the eternal verities'. The
philosophe of l. 17 are *poetae theologi-philosophi,* the clerks of
antiquity. See the remarks of T. Hunt, item 239.

427   Stemmler, Theo. 'Die mittelenglischen Bearbeitungen zweier
      Lais der Marie de France', *Anglia,* LXXX (1962), 243-63.
      Concerns the relationship between *Le Fresne* and the Middle English
      Lai le Freine, and between Lanval and *Sir Launfal.*

428   Stevens, John. 'The *granz biens* of Marie de France', in
      *Patterns of Love and Courtesy: Essays in Memory of C.S.
      Lewis.* London: Arnold, 1966, pp. 1-25.
      A general and often superficial discussion of the *Lais* with particular
      emphasis on images. The expression *granz biens* is defined as 'an ex-
      perience. Not a theory, not a moral lesson, not even an insight into
      character, but an experience of fine feeling. The experience is embodied
      in a narrative, but it comes over most forcefully in an image, or series of
      images' (p. 3).

429   —, *Medieval Romance: Themes and Approaches.* London:
      Hutchinson University Library, 1973.
      Contains a number of references to the *Lais* and an analysis of *Guigemar*
      (pp. 160-5) with stress on the images found in this *lai* (the white hind,
      the incurable wound, the magic ship, the enclosed garden).

430   Stokoe, William C., Jr. 'The Sources of *Sir Launfal: Lanval*
      and *Graelent', Publications of the Modern Language
      Association of America,* LXIII (1948), 392-404.
      A successful attempt to refute the theories of Schofield (item 405) and
      Foulet (item 176) concerning the relationship between *Graelent* and
      Lanval. In composing *Lanval* Marie worked from *Graelent* and modified
      the naive narrative of her source, displaying considerable artistic skill.

431   Sturm, Sara. *The Lay of Guingamor: a Study.* Chapel Hill:
      University of North Carolina Press (University of North
      Carolina Studies in Romance Languages and Literatures,
      LXXVI), 1968.
      Little direct reference to Marie, but a useful parallel study.

432   Suchier, Hermann and A. Birch-Hirschfeld. *Geschichte der französischen Litteratur, von den ältesten Zeiten bis zum Gegenwart.* Leipzig and Vienna: Bibliographisches Institut, 1900, 2nd ed., 1913.
Contains some influential remarks on Marie, pp. 127-8 (2nd ed., pp. 132-3).

433   Sudre, L. 'Les Allusions à la légende de Tristan dans la littérature du moyen âge', *Romania,* XV (1886), 534-57.
Pp. 551-6 deal with *Chievrefoil.* Marie's *lai* was derived from a group relating different episodes of the Tristan legend and distinguished by their brevity and musical form.

434   Taylor, A.B. *An Introduction to Medieval Romance.* London: Heath Cranton, 1930. Reprinted, New York: Barnes & Noble, 1969.
Contains a section entitled 'Breton Lays and the Lays of Marie de France' (pp. 52-6).

435   Tegethoff, Ernst. *Märchen, Schwänke und Fabeln.* Munich: Bruckmann (Bücher des Mittelalters), 1925.
Contains a translation in German prose of *Lanval,* pp. 113-18 (taken from W. Hertz, *Spielmannsbuch,* item 50) and of three of Marie's fables, *De asino adulante* (ed. Warnke, no. XV), *De mure uxorem petente* (ed. Warnke, no. LXXIII) and *De uxore mala et marito eius* (ed. Warnke, no. XCV), pp. 175-7.

436   Thiébaux, Marcelle. *The Stag of Love: the Chase in Medieval Literature.* Ithaca and London: Cornell University Press, 1974.
Pertinent background information for the white hind episode in *Guigemar* (esp. pp. 106-15).

437   Thorpe, Lewis. 'Les *Fables* de Marie de France: un nouveau fragment de manuscrit', *Scriptorium,* IV (1950), 102-4.
Offers 15 lines of the fable *De fabro et securi* (ed. Warnke, no. XLIX), from a Wollaton Hall MS now at the University of Nottingham.

438   Tiemann, Barbara. *Fabel und Emblem: Gilles Corrozet und die französische Renaissance-Fabel.* Munich: Fink (Humanistische Bibliothek, Reihe I, Abhandlungen, XVIII), 1974.
Contains a number of isolated references to Marie's *Fables* and an excellent bibliography.

439   Tiemann, H. *Die Entstehung der mittelalterlichen Novelle in*

Frankreich. Hamburg: Stiftung Europa-Kolleg, 1961.
Contains a brief consideration of Marie de France (pp. 15-18) in the context of an elucidation of the nature and origins of the French *nouvelle.*

440   Tobler, Adolf. 'Zu den *Lais* der Marie de France', *Zeitschrift für romanische Philologie,* X (1886), 164-9.
A review of Warnke, item 15. Important textual emendations.

441   Toja, Gianluigi. 'Forme di vita e"vie féerique"nei *Lais* di Maria di Francia', *Spicilegio Moderno,* I (1973), 101-18.
Discussion of Marie's use of objects and images, with stress on her powers of observation, is followed by an examination of the fairy element in the *Lais,* which erupts surprisingly in a realistic, bourgeois setting. The later part of the article is taken up by remarks on the two stylistic planes seen in the *Lais,* the narrative level in which the rhythm is slow and details are provided 'indulgently', and the level of direct action in which personages   move and speak like *dramatis personae.* Useful, but somewhat vague.

442   Toldo, Pietro. '*Yonec',* *Romanische Forschungen,* XVI (1904), 609-29.
Some superficial comments on the literary qualities of *Yonec* are followed by some additions, mainly oriental, to the source material provided by R. Köhler (item 15). *Yonec* is seen as a 'mélange singulier de paganisme et de christianisme'.

443   Trindade, W. Ann. 'The Man with Two Wives – Marie de France and an Important Irish Analogue', *Romance Philology,* XXVII (1973-4), 466-78.
A dense and interesting article. The theme of the Man with Two Wives, as identified by Gaston Paris (item 350) consists of two types of narrative pattern: (1) tales based on a simple formula of repetition or doubling; (2) the functional opposition of two ladies to the husband (as in *Le Fresne* and *Eliduc).* The modification in type 2 was probably caused by oral borrowing from Celtic tradition. *Eliduc* and *Le Fresne* may have been modelled on a Breton story similar in structure to Marie's version and entitled *Guildeluec ha Guilliadun,* a type exemplified by the Irish tale *Tochmarc Fithirné ocus Dáiriné dá Ingen Túathail,* 'The Wooing of Fithir and Dáiriné, Two Daughters of Túathail'.

444   Tyrwhitt, Thomas. *The Canterbury Tales of Chaucer, to which are added an Essay upon his Language and Versification, an Introductory Discourse and Notes.* 5 vols, London, 1775 etc.

Vol. I, pp. cc-cciii, contains what seems to be the earliest attribution to Marie of both the *Fables* and the *Lais*. Tyrwhitt considers it 'extremely probable' that Chaucer had read the *Lais*. Vol. IV, pp. 261-2, cites the epilogues to *Eliduc* and *Guigemar* and the prologue to *Chevrefoil* in an attempt to show 'how exactly Chaucer and she [Marie] agree in their manner of speaking of the Armorican bards'. Cf. Baum, item 85, pp. 69-80.

445 *Valeri, Diego. *Romanzi e racconti d'amore del medio evo francese.* Milan, 1943.
Contains a translation of *Guigemar* and *Chevrefoil* (pp. 103-29).

446 Valero, Ana-María. 'El *lai* del *Chievrefueil* de María de Francia', *Boletín de la Real Academia de Buenas Letras de Barcelona,* XXIV (1951-2), 173-83.
Discusses several points concerning the interpretation of *Chevrefoil.* Suggests unconvincingly that the form *nun* (for *nuns*) should be understood as 'message' (Latin *nuntium).* We should distinguish between *la codre* (ll. 51, 70), 'the hazel-branch' and *li codres* (l. 75), 'the hazel-tree'.
Review by:
.1 I. Frank, *Romania,* LXXV (1954), 131-2.

447 Venckeleer, Théo. *Rollant li proz: contribution à l'histoire de quelques qualifications laudatives en français du moyen âge.* Paris: Champion, 1975.
Frequent references to Marie's works.

448 Vising, P.J. *Le Purgatoire de saint Patrice des manuscrits harléien 273 et fonds français 2198,* publié pour la première fois. Gothenburg (Göteborgs Högskolas Arsskrift, XXI, 3), 1916.
The text is accompanied by cross-references to Marie's *Espurgatoire.*

449 Voretzsch, Karl. *Einführung in das Studium der altfranzösischen Literatur.* 3rd ed., Halle: Niemeyer, 1925.
Contains a useful introduction to the *Fables* (pp. 153-5) and the *Lais* (pp. 393-8; bibliography, pp. 398-9).

460 — , *Introduction to the Study of Old French Literature,* trans. Francis M. Du Mont, Halle: Niemeyer, 1931. Reprint, Geneva: Slatkine, 1976.
The *Lais* are discussed on pp. 263-6 (Bibliography, pp. 266-8), the *Fables* on pp. 128-30.

461 Walpole, Ronald N. 'Humor and People in Twelfth-Century

France', *Romance Philology*, XI (1957-8), 210-25.
Stresses Marie's sense of humour (pp. 220-1).

452   Ward, Harry L.D. *Catalogue of Romances in the Department of Manuscripts in the British Museum.* 2 vols, London, 1883-93.
Contains a description of the British Library MSS of the *Lais* (vol. I, pp. 407-15) and the *Fables* (vol. II, pp. 291-307). Also offers biographical details, remarks on each of the *lais* and a comparative table of the fables contained in the three London MSS.

453   *Warnke, Karl. *Marie de France und die anonymen Lais.* Coburg: Ostern (Prog. des Gymn. Casimirianum zu Coburg), 1892, 24pp.
Review by:
  .1   R. Zenker, *Literaturblatt für germanische und romanische Philologie*, XII (1892), cols 418-21.

454   —, 'Die Quellen des *Esope* der Marie de France', in *Festgabe für Hermann Suchier.* Halle: Niemeyer, 1900, pp. 161-284. Also in separate print, Halle: Niemeyer, 1900.
Argument analogous to that of Mall (item 318). In the first quarter of the twelfth century an English writer called Alfred, whom Marie wrongly thought to be King Alfred, produced a collection of fables, half from the *Romulus Nilanti,* the other half added by himself from both learned and popular tradition. Marie put this English collection into French for an audience different from that for which it was originally intended.
Review by:
  .1   G. Cohn, *Archiv für das Studium der neueren Sprachen und Literaturen*, CVI (1901), 426-52.

455   —, 'Die Vorlage des *Espurgatoire St. Patriz* der Marie de France', in *Philologische Studien zum 60. Geburtstag von Karl Voretzsch.* Halle, 1927, pp. 135-54.
A detailed discussion of the manuscript tradition of Henry of Saltrey's *Tractatus.*

456   —, 'Über die Zeit der Marie de France', *Zeitschrift für romanische Philologie*, IV (1880), 223-48.
A thorough discussion of Marie's *cunte Willame,* probably William Longsword, and the *nobles reis,* probably Henry II, is followed by a detailed discussion of Marie's language, which is identified as Norman. There is no difference between Marie's language and that of the *Brut* of Wace, which suggests that Marie was active in a period not much later

than that of Wace.
Review by:
.1   P. Meyer, *Romania*, X (1881), 299.

457   Warren, F.M. 'Some Features of Style in Early French
       Narrative Poetry', *Modern Philology*, III (1905-6), 179-209,
       513-40; IV (1906-7), 655-75.
       Contains some comments on Marie, esp. III, p. 28, IV, pp. 666, 668,
       672. Useful background material.

458   Warton, Thomas. *The History of English Poetry, from the
       close of the eleventh to the commencement of the eighteenth
       century. To which are prefixed two dissertations. I. On the
       origin of romantic fiction in Europe. II. On the introduction
       of learning into England.* 2 vols, London, 1774-8.
       Vol. I contains the earliest attested reference to MS Harley 978 (1st
       dissertation, p. a[2]) with quotations from the beginning and end of some
       of Marie's *Lais*. Cf. also vol. II, pp. 102-3, and Baum, item 85, pp. 67-9.

459   Wathelet-Willem, Jeanne. 'La Conception de l'amour chez
       Marie de France', *Bibliographical Bulletin of the International
       Arthurian Society*, XXI (1969), 144-5.
       Summary of a paper delivered at the IXth International Arthurian Con-
       gress, Cardiff, August 1969.

460   —, '*Equitan* dans l'œuvre de Marie de France', *Le Moyen Age*,
       LXIX (1963), 325-45.
       The text of *Equitan* is carefully examined and the conclusion reached
       that it offers a different resonance from the rest of the *Lais*. The
       difference lies in the subject matter, the presentation of the characters,
       Marie's attitude towards them and the tempo of the narrative. *Equitan*
       is perhaps an 'œuvre de début'.

461   —, 'Un Lai de Marie de France: *Les Deux Amants*', in
       Mélanges offerts à Rita Lejeune. Gembloux: Duculot, 1969,
       vol. II, pp. 1143-57.
       Marie in the *Deus Amanz* enriched a rudimentary legend by borrowing
       from works such as the *Chanson de Roland* (e.g., *Deus Amanz*, ll. 185-9
       correspond to *Roland*, ll. 1051-5) and from Ovid's account of Pyramus
       and Thisbe (cf. Segre, item 414). The French *Pyramus* may have been
       influenced by the role of the heroine in the *Deus Amanz*. The cause of
       the young man's *démesure* is *joie*, 'exaltation amoureuse', stemming
       principally from the semi-nudity of his beloved.

462   —, 'Le Mystère chez Marie de France', *Revue Belge de*

Philologie et d'Histoire, XXXIX (1961), 661-86.

Line 61 of *Lanval* ('L'eisnee portout uns bacins') is the starting point for an analysis of mysterious elements in *Lanval* and related anonymous *lais.* The shivering of the horse, the basins (the expression *uns bacins* probably indicates a pair), the towel and the proximity of water suggest that Lanval is on the threshold of the Other World.
Summary in *Bibliographical Bulletin of the International Arthurian Society,* XII (1960), 135.
Review by:

.1   A. Vàrvaro, *Studi Francesi,* XVIII (1962), 523-4.

463   —, 'Le Personnage de Guenièvre chez Marie de France', *Marche Romane,* XIII (1963), 119-31.
An analysis of *Lanval,* ll. 219 ff. The queen's initial remarks to Lanval are seen as ambiguous, but not necessarily dishonourable. Lanval, absorbed in his love for the fairy, interprets them in their most unfavourable sense and his reaction is disrespectful and discourteous. The article contains a useful study of the terms *dru* and *druerie.*
Summary in *Bibliographical Bulletin of the International Arthurian Society,* XV (1963), 138-9.

464   Watts, Thomas D., Jr and R.J. Cormier, 'Toward an Analysis of Certain *Lais* of Marie de France', *Lingua e Stile,* IX (1974), 249-56.
Baum distinguishes between *lais* with a linear structure and those with a concentric structure (item 85, pp. 167-91). The present authors stress by means of an analysis of *Le Fresne* that Marie displays an ability to handle both types of structure in one *lai.* The linear development based on narrative segments is viewed as the surface structure, the concentric or anecdotal pattern with one focal point or central image, as the deep structure. The deep structure appears in the author's use of key words, images, symbols, analogies, etc., and it is from these that one extracts the real meaning of a text.

465   Weingartner, Russell. 'Stylistic Analysis of an Anonymous Work: the Old French Lai *Guingamor',* *Modern Philology,* LXIX (1971-2), 1-9.
A study of the style of *Guingamor* against a background of Marie's style with the conclusion that Marie is probably not the author of this lay. See item 506.

466   West, G.D. *'L'uevre Salemon', Modern Language Review,* XLIX (1954), 176-82.
Marie was not the first to use the expression *l'uevre Salemon* which is

found in *Eneas, Troie, Floire et Blancheflor,* etc. The early examples suggest that *l'uevre Salemon* was a method of carving and engraving on a hard and precious material (gold, ivory, marble, etc.). The Song of Songs was not the origin of the expression as used by Marie in *Guigemar,* l. 172 (see items 72, 81, 114 and 284).

467   Whichard, Rogers D. 'A Note on the Identity of Marie de France', in *Romance Studies Presented to William Morton Dey.* Chapel Hill: University of North Carolina Press (University of North Carolina Studies in Romance Languages and Literatures, XII), 1950, pp. 177-81.
A useful note in support of Holmes' identification of Marie as the daughter of Waleran de Meulan (item 234). Waleran was also count of Beaumont and a member of a family holding lands on both sides of the Channel. His twin brother held the earldom of Leicester and a further brother became earl of Bedford. Waleran himself was also earl of Worcester, and, in spite of having formed part of a revolt against Henry I in 1123, he was by 1150 one of Henry II's chief supporters. He was present at court in 1157 and witness to the treaty with Louis in 1160. At the time of his death in 1166, Waleran's daughter, Marie de Beaumont, would have been at the most sixteen years old.

468   Williams, Elizabeth. '*Lanval* and *Sir Landevale:* a Medieval Translator and his Methods', *Leeds Studies in English,* new series, III (1969), 85-99.
The author of *Sir Landevale* recognized in *Lanval* the bones of a good folktale which he narrated forcefully and successfully. Marie's courtly poem is adapted for a less sophisticated audience.

469   Williams, Harry F. 'La Chèvre — Person or Title?', *Bibliographical Bulletin of the International Arthurian Society,* XXIV (1972), 137-41.
The name of Marie's *Chievrefoil* was confused by some unknown author, giving rise to references to a poet named La Chèvre in *D'une none tresoriere* ('Et Li Kievres qui rimer valt/L'amour de Tristan et d'Isault') and the *Roman de Renart,* Branch II ('De Tristan dont La Chievre fist').

470   Williman, Joseph P. 'The Sources and Composition of Marie's Tristan Episode', in *Studies in Honor of Tatiana Fotitch.* Washington: Catholic Univ. of America Press, 1972, pp. 115-27.
Marie combines two main sources, the body of narrations drawn from the Tristan legend, oral or written (in particular a Celtic tale of a hazel wand bearing Tristan's name in ogam script) and the extant lyric lay of

Chèvrefeuille, attributed to Tristan. They are linked by the image, invented by Marie, of the life-giving interdependence of the hazel and the woodbine.

471   Wilmotte, Maurice. 'Un Curieux Cas de plagiat littéraire: le poème de *Galeran', Bulletin de l'Académie Royale de Belgique, Classe des Lettres,* 5th series, XXIV (1928), 269-309. Also in separate print, Paris: Champion, 1928.
The author of *Galeran* cynically plagiarized Marie's *Le Fresne,* taking from her his theme, the development of the theme, details of form and even some expressions.

472   —, 'Marie de France et Chrétien de Troyes', *Romania,* LII (1926), 353-5.
Did Marie precede or follow Chrétien? The author suggests the latter and supports this with quotations from *Guigemar,* ll. 106-12, and *Eliduc,* 825ff, which are said to be based on *Cligès,* 646-52 (ed. Foerster), and *Guillaume d'Angleterre,* 2285ff. Marie is thus caught 'en flagrant délit de plagiat vis-à-vis de Chrétien'.

473   —, 'Problèmes de chronologie littéraire', *Le Moyen Age,* LIII (1940), 99-114.
Opposes Hoepffner's view (item 226) of the relationship between *Eliduc* and *Ille et Galeron.* Marie not only borrowed outrageously from *Eneas,* but she also borrowed from Gautier d'Arras, imposing her 'aimable amoralisme' on his conception of loyalty in love.

474   Wind, Bartina H. 'L'Idéologie courtoise dans les *Lais* de Marie de France', in *Mélanges de linguistique romane et de philologie médiévale offerts à M.Maurice Delbouille.* Gembloux: Duculot, 1964, vol. II, pp. 741-8.
The *Lais* contain courtly heroes, but no real courtly love. Courtly influences are superficial, the subject matter being derived from 'données légendaires, merveilleuses et traditionnelles'. *Eliduc,* seen as a 'lai anti-courtois', is taken as an example of the predominance in the *Lais* of folklore and popular beliefs.

475   Winkler, Emil. *Französische Dichter des Mittelalters. II. Marie de France.* Vienna: Hölder (Sitzungsberichte der kaiserlichen Akademie der Wissenschaften in Wien, Philosophisch-historische Klasse, CLXXXVIII), 1918.
An unsuccessful attempt to identify Marie as the Countess Marie de Champagne. No firm evidence is brought forward. Chiefly an attack on

the views of other scholars: Bédier, Mall, Suchier, Warnke, etc.
Reviews by:
.1   L. Foulet, Romania, XLIX (1923), 129-31.
.2   F.E. Guyer, *Modern Philology*, XVIII (1920-1), 171-6.
.3   F. Schürr, *Zeitschrift für französische Sprache und Literatur*, XLVI (1923), 351-8.

476   Wolf, Ferdinand J. *Über die Lais, Sequenzen und Leiche: ein Beitrag zur Geschichte der rhythmischen Formen und Singweisen der Volkslieder und der volkmässigen Kirchen- und Kunstlieder im Mittelalter*. Heidelberg, 1841, 516pp.
A wide-ranging and important study of the *lai,* but with little direct reference to Marie.

477   Woods, William, S. 'Femininity in the *Lais* of Marie de France', *Studies in Philology*, XLVII (1950), 1-19.
A largely unconvincing attempt to show that Marie displays feminine traits in both the stylistic and psychological aspects of the *Lais* (love of forceful adverbs and superlatives, fondness for exaggeration, diminutives, excessively detailed descriptions, knowledge of feminine wiles, lack of interest in war, the cruel, vindictive nature of women, etc.).

478   —, 'Marie de France's *Laüstic'*, *Romance Notes,* XII (1970-1), 203-7.
Aspects of the literary skill of Marie (understatement, use of symbols, irony, concision, symmetry, contrast, etc.) are developed by means of a study of the structure of *Laüstic.* This *lai* is divided by the author into nine sections, corresponding to lines 7-22 (the exposition), 23-38 (the plot), 39-56 (frustration), 57-78 (preparation for the conflict, present-ation of the symbol), 79-94 (the threat), 95-110 (vengeance), 111-125 (the tragic climax), 126-40 (*dénouement),* 141-56 (the lover's reaction).
Review by:
.1   G. Di Stefano, *Studi Francesi,* XLIV (1971), 322.

479   Wulff, Fr. *'Eliduc',* in *Mélanges de philologie romane dédiés à Carl Wahlund.* Macon: Protat, 1896, pp. 305-14. Reprint, Geneva: Slatkine, 1972.
Contains numerous corrections to the text of *Eliduc,* with particular reference to Warnke's 1885 edition.

480   Zimmer, H. 'Beiträge zur Namenforschung in den altfranzösischen Arthurepen', *Zeitschrift für französische Sprache und Literatur,* XIII (1891), 1-117.
Contains a discussion of the name Guigemar (pp. 1-16) and the reference to Carduel in *Lanval* (pp. 93ff.).

481   —, *'Histoire littéraire de la France,* tome **XXX**', *Göttingische gelehrete Anzeigen,* XX (1890), 785-832.

A review of item 353. The meaning of the terms *breton* and *Bretagne* in the *Lais* is discussed on pp. 796-801. The *Lais* are seen as continental in origin. See items 107, 108 and 307.

482   Zumthor, Paul. *Essai de poétique médiévale.* Paris: Editions du Seuil, 1972.

Contains an analysis of *Laüstic* from the point of view of 'fonctionnement narratif' (pp. 384-91).

IV. DISSERTATIONS

(Items in this section are doctoral dissertations, unless otherwise stated.)

483   *Allen, M.V. 'The Literary Craftsmanship of Marie de France'.
       Dissertation presented to the University of Virginia, 1954.
       Dissertation Abstracts, XIV (1954), 1714-15.

484   *Brightenback, Ebba Kristine.'Aspects of Organicity in Old
       French Romance Narrative: the Prologue and Narrative
       Modalities in the *Lais* of Marie de France. Dissertation
       presented to Princeton University. 1974, *Dissertation Abstracts,*
       XXXV (1974-5), 2931A.

485   *Brookes, Barbara S. 'A Stylistic Analysis of the *Lais* of
       Marie de France'. Dissertation presented to Columbia
       University, 1967. *Dissertation Abstracts,* XXVIII (1967-8),
       1388A-89A.

486   *Bullock-Davies, Constance. 'Marie de France and South
       Wales'. Dissertation presented to the University of Wales,
       1963.

487   *Chitwood, Garrett C., Jr. 'Love and Guilt. A Study of Suffer-
       ing in Selected Medieval Works (Marie de France, Chrétien de
       Troyes)'. Dissertation presented to Case Western Reserve
       University, 1970. *Dissertation Abstracts,* XXXI (1970-1),
       3497A-98A.

488   *Fitz, Brewster E., 'Desire and Language: Textual Metaphor
       in the *Lais* of Marie de France'. Dissertation presented to
       Yale University, 1973. *Dissertation Abstracts,* XXXIV
       (1973-4), 7189A.

489   *Genaust, Helmut. 'Die Struktur des altfranzösische anti-
       kisierenden *Lais*'. Dissertation presented to the University
       of Hamburg, 1965.

490   *Gouraige, Adrienne. 'Le Merveilleux dans les *Lais* de Marie

de France'. Dissertation presented to the State University of New York, Albany, 1973. *Dissertation Abstracts,* XXXIV (1973-4), 3394A.

491 *Green, Robert B. 'The Growth of Love: a Study of Reality and Symbolism in the *Lays* of Marie de France'. Dissertation presented to Rutgers University, 1971. *Dissertation Abstracts,* XXXII (1971-2), 3250A.

492 *Illingworth, R.N. 'A Study of the *Lais* of Marie de France and Celtic Analogues'. Dissertation presented to the University of Oxford, 1959.

493 *Jockin, Yvette. 'Essai de Chronologie des *Lais* de Marie de France'. *Mémoire* presented to the University of Liège, 1955.

494 *Johnson, Phyllis A. 'Conventions littéraires dans la poésie narrative du XIIe siècle'. Dissertation presented to the University of California at Los Angeles, 1967. *Dissertation Abstracts,* XXVIII (1967-8), 2686A.
Contains a stylistic analysis of *Guigemar* and *Chevrefoil,* stressing that Marie made extensive use of formulas and formulaic expressions.

495 *Knapton, Antoinette. 'Mythe et Psychologie chez Marie de France'. Dissertation presented to the University of California at Berkeley, 1971. *Dissertation Abstracts,* XXXII (1971-2), 2646A. See item 268.

496 *Le Mée, Katharine W. 'A Metrical Study of Five *Lais* of Marie de France'. Dissertation presented to Columbia University, 1971, 292pp. *Dissertation Abstracts,* XXXIV (1973-4), - 6618A-19A. See item 278.

497 *Lozachmeur, Jean-Claude. 'L'Imparfait de l'indicatif dans les *Lais* de Marie de France'. *Thèse de IIIe cycle* presented to the University of Rennes, 1970.

498 *Lutz, G.' Le Vocabulaire psychologique et affectif dans les *Lais* de Marie de France'. *Mémoire* presented to the Centre de philologie romane, Strasbourg, 1962.

499 *Moritz, William E. '*Guingamor, Guigemar, Graelentmor, Lanval,* and *Desiré:* a Comparative Study of Five Breton Lays'. Dissertation presented to the University of Southern

California, 1968. *Dissertation Abstracts,* XXIX (1968-9), 3582A-83A.

500 *Patton, Patricia J. *'Sir Launfal:* a Source Study'. Dissertation presented to Columbia University, 1972. *Dissertation Abstracts,* XXXIV (1973-4), 1250A-51A.

501 *Pepper, J.M. 'Courtly Conventions, 1150-1250, as shown in the Tristan Legends, in the Writings of Marie de France and in the Arthurian Legends'. M.A. thesis presented to the University of Bristol, 1961.

502 *Petricone, Sister Ancilla M., S.C. 'The Middle English Breton Lays: a Structural Analysis of Narrative Technique'. Dissertation presented to the Catholic University of America, 1973. *Dissertation Abstracts,* XXXIV (1973-4), 1251A-52A.

503 *Rosso, Joseph. 'Le Vocabulaire des *Lais* de Marie de France et son aspect social'. Dissertation presented to the University of Aix-en-Provence, 1967, xii + 271pp.

504 *Rothschild, J.R. 'Narrative Technique in the *Lais* of Marie de France: Themes and Variations'. Dissertation presented to The Johns Hopkins University, 1968. *Dissertation Abstracts,* XXIX (1968-9), 1519A. See item 390.

505 *Savage, E.B. 'Dramatic Treatments of the Tristan and Isolt Tale: A Comparative Study (Marie de France: *Chevrefoil,* R. Wagner, Jean Cocteau: *L'Eternel Retour)*'. Dissertation presented to the University of Minnesota 1959. *Dissertation Abstracts,* XX (1959-60), 4100-1. See item 400.

506 *Weingartner, Russell. 'The Authorship of the Old-French Lai *Guingamor'.* Dissertation presented to Princeton University, 1968. *Dissertation Abstracts,* XXIX (1968-9), 2688A-89A. See item 465.

507 *Wennberg, Benkt. 'Marie de France and the Anonymous *Lais:* a Study of the Narrative *Lai* in the Twelfth and Thirteenth Centuries'. Dissertation presented to the University of Pennsylvania, 1956. *Dissertation Abstracts,* XVI (1956), 2450-1.

508 Wiltshire, Ernest M. 'Recherches sur le vocabulaire courtois dans les *Lais* de Marie de France'. M.A. thesis presented to Queen's University, Kingston, Ontario, 1969.

509   *Wolf, Sister Leah, S.C. 'The Implied Author in the *Lais* of Marie de France'. Dissertation presented to the University of Pittsburgh, 1974, 145pp. *Dissertation Abstracts,* XXXV (1974-5), 1679A.

ADDENDA

Addition to existing item

20   Gumbrecht, Hans U. *Marie de France: Äsop, eingeleitet, kommentiert und übersetzt.*
Contains a bibliography (pp. 9-16), an introductory chapter entitled 'Fabeln und literaturwissenschaftliches Erkenntnisinteresse: Vorschläge zum Umgang mit dem *Esope* der Marie de France in hermeneutischer Absicht' (pp. 17-52), the text of the Prologue, 102 fables and the Epilogue with a translation into German, and an appendix on the fable *De corvo et vulpe* (no. XIII).

Anthologies

510   Bianciotto, Gabriel. *Les Poèmes de Tristan et Iseut.* Paris: Nouveaux Classiques Larousse, 1974.
Contains a text of *Chevrefoil* with an introduction, translation and philological commentary (pp. 88-99).

511   Oulmont, Charles. *La Poésie française du moyen-âge: XIe-XVe siècles*, recueil de textes accompagné de traductions, de notices et précédé d'une étude littéraire. Paris: Mercure de France, 1913.
Contains a text of *Chevrefoil* with a translation (pp. 169-74).

Translations and adaptations

512   Giduz, Hugo and Urban T. Holmes. Jr. *Sept contes de la vieille France,* illustrated by Alice M. Beyer. Boston, etc: Heath's Modern Language Series, 1930.
Modern French adaptations of *Chaitivel*, the *Deus Amanz*, *Bisclavret*, *Milun*, *Guigemar*, *Yonec* and *Eliduc.*

513   Goodrich, Norma L. *The Ways of Love: Eleven Romances from Mediæval France.* London: George Allen and Unwin, 1965.
Contains a translation of *Eliduc* (pp. 66-86) and of *Yonec* (pp. 87-97).

514   Legrand d'Aussy, Pierre-Jean-Baptiste. *Tales from the Twelfth*

and Thirteenth Centuries from the French of Mr Le Grand.
2 vols, London, 1786.
Contains a translation of *Lanval* (vol. I, pp. 1-16). Translator's name not given.

515   Williams, Edwin B. *Aucassin et Nicolette and Four Lais of Marie de France,* edited with an introduction, notes and vocabulary. New York: Crofts, 1933.
Contains modern French versions of *Chevrefoil,* the *Deus Amanz, Laüstic* and *Lanval,* aimed at the teaching of modern French.

Books and articles

516   Brush, Murray P. *The Isopo Laurenziano: edited with notes and an introduction treating of the interrelation of Italian fable collections.* Columbus, Ohio: Laurence Press, 1899.
Contains material on the relationship between Marie and the Italian collection. Chapter IV is entitled 'Collections derived from the *Fables* of Marie de France' (pp. 43-65).

517   Cohen, Gustave. *Le Roman courtois au XII siècle.* Paris: Centre de Documentation Universitaire (Les Cours de Sorbonne), 1934.
Marie is the subject of fasc. IV, pp. 139-63. Offers a general introduction to the *Lais* with particular mention of *Eliduc* (pp. 145-50), *Guigemar* (pp. 152-5) and *Lanval* (pp. 155-9). The *Lais* are divided into *lais romanesques* (*Eliduc, Le Fresne, Chevrefoil,* and the *Deus Amanz*), *lais féeriques* (*Guigemar, Lanval, Yonec,* and *Bisclavret*) and *lais fabliaux* (*Laüstic, Equitan, Chaitivel* and *Milun*).

518   Dragonetti, Roger. 'Le Lai narratif de Marie de France "pur quei fu fez, coment e dunt",' in *Littérature, Histoire, linguistique: recueil d'études offert à Bernard Gagnebin.* Lausanne: L'Age d'Homme, 1973, pp. 31-53.
Marie's narrative *lais* are considered as metaphorical developments from earlier musical *lais,* whose memory is preserved in the narrative, the authenticity of which is guaranteed by its ancient origin. The author analyses the Prologue, in which the *noble reis* (1. 43) is seen more as God than as a real king, as an aesthetic manifesto relating divine and monarchic authority to the moral and aesthetic aspects of composition. He examines the metaphorical development of commemoration and the role attributed to the king/God, in *Bisclavret, Chaitivel, Chevrefoil* and *Eliduc.*

519   Gidel, C. 'Marie de France', *Revue Historique de l'Anjou,* I

(1886), 405-32.

A general appreciation of the *Lais,* the *Fables* and the *Espurgatoire.* Of little interest.

520 Gullberg, Gotthard. *Mémoire grammatical sur les poésies de Marie de France.* Copenhagen: Ferslew, 1874, 48pp.

Deals principally with Marie's use of verbs. Superficial.

521 Hodgson, Frederick. 'Alienation and the Otherworld in *Lanval, Yonec,* and *Guigemar', Comitatus,* V (1974), 19-31.

Aims at demonstrating the importance for Marie's art of the *merveilleux celtique.* Lanval, the lady in *Yonec,* Guigemar and his lady are caught in a 'loveless plight' and alienated from social reality. The Otherworld offers a means by which social circumstances can be transcended, providing an alternative reality. Marie's use of the Otherworld motif evolves in a way which suggests the order of composition *Lanval, Yonec, Guigemar.*

522 Jauffret, Louis-François. *Lettres sur les fabulistes anciens et modernes.* 3 vols, Paris: Pichon-Béchet, 1827.

Marie's *Fables* are the subject of letters XXXIV-XXXVIII (vol. I, pp. 179-204). Offers a general introduction with examples. The *Fables* are seen as dedicated to Guillaume de Dampierre.

523 Keidel, George, C. *Old French Fables: the Interrupted Work of the Late Professor Elliott.* Baltimore, 1910, 4 pp.

Mentions the projected edition of the *Fables* by Prof. Aaron M. Elliott. Offers general but useful remarks on the content of the *Fables.*

524 Krömer, Wolfram. *Kurzerzählungen und Novellen in den romanischen Literaturen bis 1700.* Berlin: Schmidt (Grundlagen der Romanistik, III), 1973.

A short section devoted to the *lai* (pp. 35-47) makes substantial reference to Marie. References elswhere in the text relate Marie to the short story tradition.

525 Lakits, Pál. *A Kaland Változásai az ófrancia udvari novella történetéhez.* Budapest: Akadémiai Kiadó (Modern filológiai füzetek, II), 1967.

Contains three chapters with particular reference to Marie : chapter II, 'Az *aventure* jelentése Marie de France novelláiban' (pp. 17-24); chapter III, 'A kaland jellege és szerepe Marie de France novelláiban' (pp. 25-49); chapter IV, 'A kaland Marie de France követoinél' (pp. 50-3).

526 Pastine, Luigi. 'Les Lais bretons et la légende de Tristan', *Nouvelle Revue d'Italie,* XIX (1922), 452-9.

General remarks on the relation of Marie to earlier Breton *lais*. Discusses the views of Foulet (esp. item 176) and Levi (item 296).

527   Richomme, Florent. 'Essai sur les *Lais* de Marie de France', *Bulletin de la Société d'Agriculture, Sciences et Arts de la Sarthe,* 2nd series, IX (1863-4), 524-34.

Attempts to 'faire connaître et gouter les lais, trop peu lus, de Marie de France' (p. 527), in particular with extracts from *Guigemar* (pp. 527-32) and *Yonec* (pp. 532-3).

528   —, 'Etude littéraire des *Fables* de Marie de France, poète du XIIIe siècle', *Bulletin de la Société d'Agriculture, Sciences et Arts de la Sarthe,* 2nd series, VIII (1861-2), 642-70.

A useful general introduction to the *Fables* with a number of complete examples in partially modernized versions. Concludes that: 'Dans ses petites compositions, le moraliste reprend toujours la parole après le conteur' (p. 644).

529   Roquefort, B. de. *De l'état de la poésie françoise dans les XIIe et XIIIe siècles.* Paris: Fournier, 1815.

Contains several references to Marie (pp. 47, 198-9, 219-20) and offers the text of three fables, *De lupo et agno* (ed. Warnke, no. II), *De corvo et vulpe* (ed. Warnke, no. XIII) and *De rustico et monedula eius* (ed. Warnke, no. LVI), pp. 352-61.

INDEX OF MARIE DE FRANCE'S WORKS

Items listed here are intended as a guide to research on a particular composition by Marie. For the general prologue to the Lais or an individual lai, studies in section (a) relate directly to the subject concerned. Those in section (b) contain useful additional material in a wider context. Page references, where appropriate, are given in parentheses. When an item has been published in more than one place, page references are to the first location only. Complete books devoted to Marie (see p. 29), notes to editions, or reviews, are not normally listed in this appendix.

The *Lais*, general prologue

Text

Battaglia, 1; Ewert, 2; Hoepffner, 5; Linker, 7; Lods, 8; Mölk, 35; Neri, 10; Richthofen, 11; Roquefort, 12; Rychner, 13; Warnke, 15, 16, 17, 18.

Translations

Battaglia, 1; Ewert, 2 (163); Hertz, 49; Jonin, 51; Neri, 10; Roquefort, 12; Warnke, 15 (225), 16, 17 (259).

Studies

(a) Brightenback, 102; Donovan, 152; Fitz, 170; Hunt, 239; Mickel, 334; D.W. Robertson, Jr., 386; Spitzer, 426.

(b) Cohn, 16.1 (30-2); Damon, 139 (975-7); Delbouille, 147; Dragonetti, 158 (32-8); Foulet, 176; Frappier, 191 (606); Levi, 298 (681-2); Riquer, 383 (13-15); Schober, 402 (54); Skårup, 416; Spitzer, 423 (238ff.); Stevens, 428 (1), 429 (211-12).

Guigemar

Text

Battaglia, 1; De Bernardi, 2; Ewert, 3; Harris, 4; Hoepffner, 5; Linker, 7; Lods, 8; Neri, 10; Pauphilet, 37; Roquefort, 12; Rychner, 13; Warnke, 15, 16, 17.

Translations and adaptations

Battaglia, 1; Frappier, 48; Giduz and Holmes, 512; Hertz, 49; Jonin, 51; Lebesgue, 54; Legrand d'Aussy, 55, 56, 57; Mason, 59, 60; Moréas, 61; Neri, 10; Reeves, 63; Rickert, 64; Roquefort, 12; Tuffrau, 67; Valeri, 445; Way, 69; H.F. Williams, 71.

Studies

(a) Abercrombie, 72; Brown, 105; Bullock-Davies, 114; Delbouille, 147; Green, 204; Holmes, 236; Illingworth, 240; Knapton, 268; Laurie, 283; Lawton, 284;

Lods, 304; Neri, 338; Pickens, 362, 363; West, 466.

(b) Bar, 81 (157-60); Bédier, 89 (835 ff.); Brereton, 101; Bromwich, 103 (462-3), 104; Brightenback, 102; Bruce, 106 (I, 53-6); Bullock-Davies, 110 (29); Cigada, 123 (22-4); Clédat, 125 (161-5); Cohen 517 (152-5); Cohn, 16.1 (26-7); Conigliani, 129 (284, 289-91); Crosland, 135 (97); Damon, 139 (978-83); Delbouille, 147; Ferguson, 166 (12-13); Foulet, 176, 178; Foulon, 182 (255); Frappier, 191 (605-6); Frey, 193 (7-8, 13); Fuchs, 196 (14-25); Hodgson, 521 (26-8); Hoepffner, 216 (1934 vol., 45-65), 218 (16-19), 223 (279-88), 224 (6-7, 15, etc.), 225 (15-20), 228 (85-7, 93); Hofer, 229 (411-14, 419); Holmes, 233 (186-7); Illingworth, 242; Johnson, 494; O.M. Johnston, 253 (327-8); Kemp-Welch, 262 (41-3); Klingender, 267 (482); Knapton, 269; Koubichkine, 271 (483 ff.); Lazar, 285 (189-93); Leach, 286 (206-8), 287 (205-6); Lejeune, 293 (40); Lot, 306 (514); Loth, 306. 1 (479), 310 (481); Meissner, 326 (265-70); Ménard, 327 (37); Mickel, 332 (273-4, 275-6, 278-9, 287-8), 333 (43-6); Moritz, 499; Neri, 10 (389-97); Newstead, 339 (930-1); Ogle, 345 (391-3); Paton, 355 (65 ff.); Payen, 358 (325-8); Pelan, 360 (113, 117-21, 123); Pollmann, 365 (317-19); Reinhard, 373 (329-30); Richomme, 527 (527-32); Roulleau, 392 (29-30); Schober, 402 (46-8); Schürr, 407 (371-2), 409 (559-61); Segre, 414 (846); Skårup, 416; Spitzer, 425 (29-30, etc.); Stevens, 429 (160-5); Thiébaux, 436 (106-15); Walpole, 451 (220); Wilmotte, 472, 473 (110-12); Zimmer, 480 (1-16), 481 (787).

Equitan

Text

Battaglia, 1; Ewert, 3; Hoepffner, 5; Linker, 7; Lods, 8; Neri, 10; Roquefort, 12; Rychner, 13; Warnke, 15, 16, 17.

Translations and adaptations

Battaglia, 1; Ellis, 45, 46a; Hertz, 49; Jonin, 51; Mason, 59; Neri, 10; Roquefort, 12; H.F. Williams, 71.

Studies

(a) Delbouille, 148; Green, 203; Hoepffner, 220; Pickens, 362; D.W. Robertson, Jr., 385; Wathelet-Willem, 460.

(b) Bayrav, 87 (71); Bédier, 89 (855, 857); Bruce, 106 (II, 176); Brugger, 107 (142-4); Clédat, 125 (166-9); Cohn, 16.1 (18, 20); Conigliani, 129 (286-7, 290-1); Crosland, 135 (97-8); Damon, 139 (971); Delbouille, 147 (193); Ferguson, 166 (13-4); Frappier, 191 (606-7); Frey, 193 (6-7, 9, 14); Hatcher, 210 (339); Hoepffner, 218 (4-5), 223 (302-3), 224 (16), 228 (89-90); Hofer, 229 (409-11, 416); Illingworth, 242; Lazar, 285 (194-6); Leach, 286 (208), 287 (206); Lot, 306 (526), 307 (39-40, note 5); Ménard, 327 (37-8); Mickel, 332 (267-70, 274, 284-6, 289), 333 (46-8); Payen, 358 (318-20); Pelan, 360 (120-1); Pollmann, 365 (310-6), Rothschild, 390 (21-47); Schürr, 409 (561); Schofield, 404 (426-8); Spitzer, 425 (36); Stevens, 428 (17-18); Watts and Cormier, 464 (255-6); Zimmer, 481 (797-8).

Le Fresne

Text

Battaglia, 1; Ewert, 3; Hoepffner, 5; Linker, 7; Lods, 8; Neri, 10; Roquefort, 12; Rychner, 13; Warnke, 15, 16, 17.

Translations and adaptations

Battaglia, 1; Ellis, 46, 46a; Hertz, 49, 50; Jonin, 51; Luquiens, 58; Mason, 59, 60; Moréas, 61; Neri, 10; Reeves, 63; Rickert, 64; Roquefort, 12; Tuffrau, 67; H.F. Williams, 71.

Studies

(a) Adler, 74; Küchler, 274; Nagel, 337; Stemmler, 427.

(b) Adler, 75; Bayrav, 87 (70-1); Bédier, 89 (853, 855); Brereton, 101; Bruce, 106 (I, 63; II, 176); Clédat, 125 (169-71); Cohn, 16.1 (21-2); Crosland, 135 (98); Damon, 139 (971-2); Ferguson, 166 (14); Francis, 186 (91-3); Frappier, 191 (607); Frey, 193 (8, 10, 14-15); Gidel, 519 (414-15), Hatcher, 210 (339); Hirsh, 214; Hoepffner, 218 (3-4), 222, 225 (37-9), 227 (14-17), 228 (90-3); Holmes, 232 (337-8), 233 (187-8); Kemp-Welch, 262 (38-9); Knapton, 269; Koubichkine, 271 (468-9); Leach, 286 (208), 287 (206); Lejeune, 293 (40); Levi, 297; Mickel, 332 (275), 333 (48-50); Matzke, 324; Payen, 358 (328-9); Pelan, 360 (118-19); Rothschild, 390 (48-91), Schürr, 407 (372-3), 409 (561-2); Spitzer, 425 (35-6, 47); Trindade, 443 (469-76); Watts and Cormier, 464 (252-5); Wilmotte, 471.

Bisclavret

Text

Bartsch, 28; Battaglia, 1; Ewert, 3; Hoepffner, 5; Linker, 7; Lods, 8; Neri, 10; Richthofen, 11; Roquefort, 12; Rychner, 13; Voretzsch, 42; Warnke, 15, 16, 17, 18.

Translations and adaptations

Battaglia, 1; Costello, 45; Ellis, 46, 46a; Giduz and Holmes, 512; Hertz, 49; Jonin, 51; Koulakovski, 52; Mason, 59, 60; Neri, 10; Reeves, 63; Roquefort, 12; Tuffrau, 67; Weston, 70; H.F. Williams, 71.

Studies

(a) Bambeck, 79; Battaglia, 84; Chotzen, 122; Loth, 309; Rothschild, 391.

(b) Bosquet, 100 (239-43); Brereton, 101; Bruce, 106 (I, 62-3; II, 176, 179); Clédat, 125 (171-2); Crosland, 135 (98); Damon, 139 (977-8); Dragonetti, 518 (39-40); Dunn, 156; Eberwein, 161 (42-5); Ferguson, 166 (5); Frappier, 191 (607); Frey, 193 (9); Grimes, 206 (32-7); Hertz, 212 (90-3); Hoepffner, 218 (4), 224 (8-9), 228 (87-8); Holmes, 233 (187); Jubainville, 265.1 (324-5); Kittredge, 265; Lazar, 285 (194); Leach, 286 (208-15), 287 (206-7); Lot, 306 (515), Loth, 306.1 (479), 310 (481); McKeehan, 313 (796-802); Mickel, 332 (279-80), 333 (50-1); Paris, 352 (44, 79); Payen, 358 (329); Pelan, 360 (122); Reinhard and Hull, 370 (52 ff.); Riquer, 383 (7-8); Rohlfs, 388 (96-213); Rothschild, 390 (92-138); Savage, 399 (149-50); Schürr, 407 (373), 409 (562); K.F. Smith,

418 (11-13); Spitzer, 425 (34); Watts and Cormier, 464 (255); Zimmer, 481 (799-800).

Lanval

Text

Battaglia, 1; Erling, 30; Ewert, 3; Harris, 4; Hoepffner, 5; Linker, 7; Lods, 8; Mercatanti, 9; Neri, 10; Palfrey and Holbrook, 36; Pauphilet, 37; Roquefort, 12; Rychner, 13, Rychner and Aebischer, 14; Warnke, 15, 16, 17, 18.

Translations and adaptations

Battaglia, 1; Hertz, 49, 50; Jonin, 51; Lebesgue, 54; Legrand d'Aussy, 55, 56, 57, 514; Levy, 299; Luquiens, 58; Mason, 59, 60; Neri, 10; Reeves, 63; Roquefort, 12; Tegethoff, 435; Tuffrau, 67; Way, 69; Weston, 70; E.B. Williams, 515; H.F. Williams, 71.

Studies

(a) Bullock-Davies, 111; Burger, 115; Cross, 136; Davison, 142; Francis, 187; Hoepffner, 219; Koubichkine, 271; Levi, 299; Maraud, 320; Marchiori, 321; O'Sharkey, 346; Rothschild, 391; Schofield, 406; Segre, 413; Stemmler, 427; Stokoe, 430; Wathelet-Willem, 463; H.F. Williams, 468.

(b) Adler, 75; Bar, 81; Bédier, 89 (856); Bliss, 96, 97; Boiron and Payen, 99 (21-2); Brereton, 101; Bromwich, 103 (461, 467); Bruce, 106 (II, 176-7, 179-80); Brugger, 107 (121-4); Clédat, 124 (291-4), 125 (172-8); Cohen, 517 (155-9); Cohn, 16.1 (19-20); Crosland, 135 (95-6); Cross, 137; Damon, 139 (973, 983-6); Duval, 159 (716-20); Eberwein, 161 (45 ff.); Ferguson, 166 (15-16); Foulet, 178; Francis, 186 (86-90, 93-5); Frappier, 191 (607-8); Frey, 193 (8, 10); Galliot, 198 (140-9); Gidel, 519 (411-14); Grimes, 206; Hodgson, 521 (20-3); Hoepffner, 215 (118-19), 216 (1933 vol., 351-70), 218 (19-25), 222, 223, 224 (7, 11-16, etc.), 225 (30), 228 (1-7, 92); Hofer, 229 (414-6, 419-20); Holmes, 233 (187); Illingworth, 243; Kittredge, 266; Knapton, 269; Kolls, 270; Lakits, 277; Lazar, 285 (175-8); Leach, 286 (215-6), 287 (210); Lejeune, 293 (40); Lot, 306 (518-20); 307 (27-41); Loth, 310 (481); Mickel, 332 (282, 288-9), 333 (51-2); Meissner, 326 (273-4); Ménard, 327 (36-7); Moritz, 499; Newstead, 339; Patton, 500; Payen, 358 (308-12); Pelan, 360 (105-10, 125); Prettyman, 368; Reinhard, 373 (240 ff.); H.S. Robertson, 387; Schober, 402 (52-3); Schofield, 404 (428-31), 405; Schürr, 407 (373-4), 409 (562-5); Smithers, 420 (62-5); Spitzer, 425 (30-1); Stevens, 428 (15-16); Wathelet-Willem, 462; Zimmer, 480 (93 ff.), 481 (798-9).

Deus Amanz

Text

Battaglia, 1; Durdan, 158; Ewert, 3; Hoepffner, 5; Ideler, 33; Linker, 7; Lods, 8; Neri, 10; Roquefort, 12; Rychner, 13; St. Clair, 395; Studer and Waters, 41; Warnke, 15, 16, 17.

Translations and adaptations
Battaglia, 1; Bianchini, 94; Cohen, 44; Durdan, 158; Ellis, 46, 46a; Giduz and Holmes, 512; Hertz, 49, 50; Jonin, 51; Luquiens, 58; Mason, 59, 60; Neri, 10; O'Shaughnessy, 62; Rickert, 64; Roquefort, 12; St. Clair, 395; Terry, 66; Tuffrau, 67; E.B. Williams, 515; H.F. Williams, 71.

Studies
(a) Cohen, 127; Durdan, 158; Fasciano, 164; O.M. Johnston, 252; Lyons, 312; Noomen, 341; St. Clair, 395; Wathelet-Willem, 461.
(b) Bayrav, 87 (71-2); Bédier, 89 (854); Bruce, 106 (I, 63; II, 177, 180); Clédat, 124 (286-8), 125 (178-80); Cohen, 128 (114-6); Cohn, 16.1 (23); Crosland, 135 (99); Damon, 139 (971); De Feo, 144 (207-11); Ferguson, 166 (16-17); Francis, 186 (91); Frey, 193 (9, 14); Gidel, 519 (415-16); Hatcher, 210 (339); Hoepffner, 218 (5-6), 225 (30), 228 (88-90); Hofer, 229 (416-17); Holmes, 232 (338-9); Kemp-Welch, 262 (43-5); Lazar, 285 (183-4); Leach, 286 (224), 287 (208); Lejeune, 293 (40); Lot, 307 (43-4); Meissner, 326 (272-3); Mickel, 332 (276-7, 281, 286-7), 333 (52-4); Pelan, 360 (112, 118, 121); Rothschild, 390 (139-67); Sainte-Beuve, 145 (545-8); Schober, 402 (47-8); Schofield, 404 (417, 425-6); Schürr, 407 (374), 409 (563); Segre, 414 (846-8); Spitzer, 425 (33-4); Stevens, 428 (2-3, 6-7); Zimmer, 481 (799).

Yonec

Text
Battaglia, 1; Ewert, 3; Harris, 4; Hoepffner, 5; Linker, 7; Lods, 8; Neri, 10; Roquefort, 12; Rychner, 13; Warnke, 15, 16, 17.
Translations and adaptations
Battaglia, 1; Ellis, 46, 46a; Giduz and Holmes, 512; Goodrich, 513; Hertz, 49, 50; Jonin, 51; Lebesgue, 54; Mason, 59, 60; Moréas, 61; Neri, 10; O'Shaughnessy, 62; Reeves, 63; Rickert, 64; Roquefort, 12; Tuffrau, 67; H.F. Williams, 71.
Studies
(a) Cross, 138; Holmes, 235; Honeycutt, 238; Illingworth, 241; O.M. Johnston, 253, 254; Ogle, 344; Payen, 359; Toldo, 442.
(b) Bédier, 89 (856, 858); Brereton, 101; Bruce, 106 (II, 177-8, 180-1); Brugger, 107 (125-8); Bullock-Davies, 112 (24-7); Clédat, 124 (288-91), 125 (180-5); Cohn, 16.1 (19, 27-8); Conigliani, 129 (288); Crosland, 135 (102); Damon, 139 (990-3); De Feo, 144 (211-14); Delbouille, 147 (193); Ferguson, 166 (17-18); Frappier, 191 (608); Frey, 193 (9); Freymond, 194 (167); Hodgson, 521 (23-6); Hoepffner, 216 (1934 vol., 36-45), 218 (27-30), 223, 224 (5, 27-9), 225 (26 ff.), 228 (7-10); Hofer, 229 (418-20); Holmes, 233 (188); Kemp-Welch, 262 (45-6); Knapton, 269; Krappe, 272; Lazar, 285 (178-82); Leach, 286 (215), 287 (210); Lejeune, 293 (39); Levi, 297; Lot, 306 (520), 307 (25-41); Lyons, 311; Meissner, 326 (274-5); Mickel, 332 (282-3), 333 (54-5); Pelan, 360 (113, 117-18); Richomme, 527 (532-3); H.S. Robertson, 387; Rothschild, 390 (168-210); Schürr, 407 (374-6), 409 (563-4); Smithers, 420 (66); Spitzer, 425 (32); Stevens, 428

(7-10), 429 (113-15).

Laüstic

Text

Battaglia, 1; Bartsch and Wiese, 29; Ewert, 3; Groult, Emond and Muraille, 31; Henry, 32; Hoepffner, 5; Linker, 7; Lods, 8; Neri, 10; Pauphilet, 37; Richthofen, 11; Roncaglia, 40; Roquefort, 12; Rychner, 13; Warnke, 15, 16, 17, 18.

Translations and adaptations

Battaglia, 1; Ellis, 46, 46a; Frappier, 48; Jonin, 51; Koulakovski, 52; Lebesgue, 54; Mason, 59, 60; Neri, 10; O'Shaughnessy, 62; Reeves, 63; Rickert, 64; Roncaglia, 40; Roquefort, 12; Terry, 66; Tuffrau, 67; E.B. Williams, 515; H.F. Williams, 71.

Studies

(a) Cargo, 119; Cottrell, 133; Green, 205; Ribard, 378; Woods, 478.

(b) Bar, 81; Bédier, 89 (858); Bruce, 106 (I, 63; II, 178); Clédat, 124 (286), 125 (185-6); Cohn, 16.1 (32-8); Conigliani, 129 (288-9); Crosland, 135 (102); Damon, 139 (970); De Feo, 144 (214-15); Eberwein, 161 (35-41); Ferguson, 166 (16-17); Foulon, 182 (254); Frappier, 191 (608); Frey, 193 (4, 9-10, 15-16); Hatcher, 210 (339-40); Hoepffner, 223, 225 (32 ff.), 228 (93); Honeycutt, 237; Lazar, 285 (184-6); Leach, 286 (215-16), 287 (208); Lejeune, 293 (40); Loth, 310 (481); Lyons, 311; Meissner, 326 (271); Mickel, 332 (277-8), 333 (55-6); Nolting-Hauff, 340 (27-9); Pelan, 360 (119, 122); Savage, 399 (148-50); Schürr, 407 (376), 409 (564); Segre, 414 (848-53); Shippey, 415 (51-2); Stevens, 428 (3-5); Watts and Cormier, 464 (256); Zimmer, 481 (800-1); Zumthor, 482 (384-91).

Milun

Text

Battaglia, 1; Ewert, 3; Hoepffner, 5; Linker, 7; Lods, 8; Neri, 10; Roquefort, 12; Rychner, 13; Warnke, 15, 16, 17.

Translations and adaptations

Battaglia, 1; Ellis, 46, 46a; Giduz and Holmes, 512; Hertz, 49; Jonin, 51; Mason, 59, 60; Neri, 10; Roquefort, 12; Tuffrau, 67; H.F. Williams, 71.

Studies

(a) Bullock-Davies, 112; Green, 204.

(b) Brereton, 101; Bruce, 106 (II, 178, 181); Brugger, 107 (128-30); Chotzen, 122 (43); Clédat, 125 (186-9); Cohn, 16.1 (18-19, 23-5, 27-9); Crosland, 135 (101-2); Damon, 139 (971-2, 992); Delbouille, 147 (194); Ferguson, 166 (18-19); Francis, 185 (144), 186 (90-3); Frappier, 191 (608-9); Frey, 193 (8, 10); Hoepffner, 218 (6-13), 223 (275-7), 228 (88-9); Hofer, 229 (417); Holmes, 233 (188), Koubichkine, 271 (468); Leach, 286 (216), 287 (209); Lejeune, 293 (40); Lot, 306 (521); Lyons, 311; Meissner, 326 (275-6); Mickel, 333 (56-8);

Newstead, 339 (930-1); Pelan, 360 (110-11, 122); Potter, 366 (47-8); Riquer, 383 (9); Rothschild, 390 (211-50); Schürr, 407 (376-7), 409 (564); Smithers, 420 (75-6); Spitzer, 425 (34).

Chaitivel

Text
Battaglia, 1; Ewert, 3; Hoepffner, 5; Linker, 7; Lods, 8; Neri, 10; Roquefort, 12; Rychner, 13; Warnke, 15, 16, 17.
Translations and adaptations
Battaglia, 1; Ellis, 46, 46a; Giduz and Holmes, 512; Jonin, 51; Mason, 59, 60; Neri, 10; O'Shaughnessy, 62; Roquefort, 12; St. Clair, 65; H.F. Williams, 71.
Studies
(a) Cowling, 134; Green, 203.
(b) Brereton, 101; Bruce, 106 (II, 178); Clédat, 125 (189-91); Cohn, 16.1 (38-51); Conigliani, 129 (288); Crosland, 135 (99-100); Damon, 139 (970-1); Dragonetti, 518 (40-2); Ferguson, 166 (19); Frappier, 191 (609); Frey, 193 (8-10); Hoepffner, 225 (21); Lazar, 285 (196-8); Leach, 286 (216), 287 (208); Lejeune, 293 (40); Meissner, 326 (271-2); Mickel, 332 (270-2, 289-90), 333 (58-60); Nolting-Hauff, 340 (31-2); Payen, 358 (324); Pelan, 360 (119, 122); Philipot and Loth, 361 (333-4); Pollmann, 365 (316-17); Riquer, 383 (10-13); St. Clair, 65; Schober, 402 (47); Schürr, 407 (377-8), 409 (564-5); Spitzer, 425 (37-8); Stevens, 428 (18-21).

Chevrefoil

Text
Battaglia, 1; Bianciotto, 510; Ewert, 3; Hoepffner, 5; Linker, 7; Lods, 8; Michel, 34; Neri, 10; Palfrey and Holbrook, 36; Pauphilet, 37; Payen, 38; Pottier, 39; Richthofen, 11; Roquefort, 12; Rychner, 13; Warnke, 15, 16, 17, 18.
Translations and adaptations
Battaglia, 1; Bianciotto, 510; Costello, 45; Frappier, 48; Hertz, 49; Jonin, 51; Koulakovski, 52; Lancaster, 53; Lebesgue, 54; Legge, 290; Mason, 59, 60; Moréas, 61; Neri, 10; Oulmont, 511; Ranke, 370; Rickert, 64; Roquefort, 12; Terry, 66; Tuffrau, 67; Valeri, 445; E.B. Williams, 515; H.F. Williams, 71.
Studies
(a) Adams and Hemming, 73; Cagnon, 117; Cocito, 126; Delbouille, 146; Durand-Monti, 157; Foulet, 181; Francis, 185; Frank, 188; Frappier, 190; Hatcher, 210; Hoepffner, 217; Hofer, 230; Kamber, 259; Le Gentil, 289; Maillard, 315; Martineau-Génieys, 322; Mermier, 330; Murrell, 355; Ribard, 377; Savage, 399; Schoepperle, 403; Spitzer, 424; Valero, 446; H.F. Williams, 469; Williman, 470.
(b) Bayrav, 87 (66-70); Becker, 88 (260-3); Bédier, 89 (836, 850); Brereton, 101; Bruce, 106 (II, 178, 181-2); Brugger, 107 (132-8); Clédat, 124 (285), 125 (191-2); Conigliani, 129 (288); Crosland, 135 (93-4, 99); Damon, 139 (970); Dragonetti, 518 (43-51); Ferguson, 166 (19); Foulet, 178 (273-86); Frappier, 191

(609-13); Frey, 193 (9); Gennrich, 199 (39 ff.); Golther, 200 (221-3), 201 (43-4); Hoepffner, 215 (117-18); 218 (25-7); 225 (22), 227 (18-21); 228 (87); Hofer, 229 (420); Jodogne, 250; Johnson, 494; Kelemina, 261; Kemp-Welch, 262 (39-40); Lazar, 285 (182-3); Leach, 286 (216), 287 (209-10); Lejeune, 293 (40); Levi, 296 (135-48); Maillard, 314 (67-8); Mickel, 333 (60-1); Nolting-Hauff, 340 (27-31); Pastine, 526 (452-4), 458); Pelan, 360 (122); Ranke, 370 (97-101); Riquer, 383 (11-13); Sainte-Beuve, 145 (548-9); Savage, 400 (11-33), 505; Schürr, 407 (378); Spitzer, 425 (32); Sudre, 433 (551-6).

Eliduc

Text

Battaglia, 1; Ewert, 3; Hoepffner, 5; Levi, 6; Linker, 7; Lods, 8; Neri, 10; Roquefort, 12; Rychner, 13; Warnke, 15, 16, 17.

Translations and adaptations

Battaglia, 1; Capone, 118; Ellis, 46, 46a; Fowles, 47; Giduz and Holmes, 512; Goodrich, 513; Hertz, 49, 50; Jonin, 51; Lebesgue, 54; Levi, 6, 295; Mason, 59, 60; Moréas, 61; Neri, 10; O'Shaughnessy, 62; Rickert, 64; Roquefort, 12; Terry, 66; Tuffrau, 67; H.F. Williams, 71.

Studies

(a) Bambeck, 80; Basset, 82; De Caluwé, 143; Fitz, 171; Hoepffner, 226; Levi, 295; Matzke, 324; Nutt, 342; Paris, 350; H.S. Robertson, 387; Trindade, 443; Wulff, 479.

(b) Adler, 75; Bar, 81; Bédier, 89 (837); Brereton, 101; Bromwich, 104; Bruce, 106 (II, 178-9, 182); Clédat, 124 (294-302), 125 (192-205); Cohen, 517 (145-50); Cohn, 16.1 (52-73); Coppin, 132 (69-70); Crosland, 135 (92-3); Damon, 139 (970-1); De Feo, 144 (215-26); Dragonetti, 518 (51-3); Ferguson, 166 (20); Frappier, 189 (443), 191 (613); Frey, 193 (8, 13); Freymond, 194 (165-7); Galliot, 198 (150-7); Hoepffner, 17.2 (147-9), 218 (13-15), 223 (288-302), 225 (39-47), 227 (9-12); Hofer, 229 (418, 420); Holmes, 232 (336-7); Kemp-Welch, 262 (47-55); Lazar, 285 (186-9); Lejeune, 293 (39); Levi, 296, 297, 298 (670-9); Loth, 310 (481); Matzke, 325; Mickel, 332 (272-3), 333 (61-4); Paris, 352 (47); Payen, 358 (312-18); Pelan, 360 (111-12, 114-16, 118); Renzi, 376; Schober, 402 (49-52); Schofield, 404 (431-2); Schürr, 407 (378-80), 409 (565-6); Spitzer, 425 (31-2); Stevens, 428 (21-4); Wilmotte, 472, 473 (110, etc.); Wind, 474 (745-8); Zimmer, 481 (799).

Fables

Text (original and modernized)

Auguis, 27; Bartsch, 28; Bartsch and Wiese, 29; Ewert and Johnston, 19; Jauffret. 522; Groult, Emond and Muraille, 31; Gumbrecht, 20; Henry, 32; Ideler, 33; Legrand d'Aussy, 55, 56, 57; Mölk, 35; Richomme, 528; Roquefort, 12, 529; Voretzsch, 42; Voyer d'Argenson, 68; Warnke, 21, 22.

INDEX OF SCHOLARS AND TRANSLATORS

Numbers in parentheses relate to item summaries

Stefenelli, A., 13.9
Stemmler, T., 427
Stevens, J., 428, 429
Stokoe, W.C., Jr., 430
Studer, P., 41
Sturm, S., 431
Suchier, H., 432 (475)
Sudre, L., 244.1, 433

Tatarkiewicz, A., 43
Taylor, A.B., 434
Tegethoff, E., 435
Terry, P., 66
Thiébaux, M., 436
Thorpe, L., 437
Tiemann, B., 438
Tiemann, H., 439
Tobler, A., 15.4, 440
Toja, G., 441
Toldo, P., 442
Trindade, W.A., 443 (324)
Tuffrau, P., 67
Tyrwhitt, T., 444

Unger, C.R., 263

Valeri, D., 445
Valero, A.-M., 446
Vàrvaro, A., 8.3, 462.1
Venckeleer, T., 447
Vernay, P., 380.6
Vising, P.J., 448
Voretzsch, K., 26.1, 42, 449, 450
Voyer d'Argenson, M.-A.-R. de, 68

Wallensköld, A., 6.3, 297.2
Walpole, R.N., 451
Ward, H.L.D., 452
Warnke, K., 15, 16, 17, 18, 21, 22, 24.2, 26,
    453, 454, 455, 456 (148, 475, 479)
Warren, F.M., 457
Warton, T., 458
Waters, E.G.R., 41
Wathelet-Willem, J., 459, 460, 461, 462, 463
Watkins, J.H., 59.2
Watts, T.D., Jr., 464
Way, G.L., 69
Weerenbeck, B.H.J., 4.1
Weingartner, R., 465
Wennberg, B., 507
West, G.D., 466

Weston, J.L., 70 (396)
Whichard, R.D., 467
Wiese, L., 29
Williams, E., 468
Williams, E.B., 515
Williams, H.F., 71, 469
Williman, J.P., 470
Wilmotte, M., 15.5, 471, 472, 473
Wiltshire, E.M., 508
Wind, B.H., 474
Winkler, E., 475
Wolf, F., 476
Wolf, L., 509 (371)
Woods, W.S., 477, 478
Wulff, Fr., 479

Zenker, R., 455.1
Zimmer, H., 353.1, 480, 481 (77)
Zumthor, P., 380.7, 482

INDEX OF GEOGRAPHICAL, HISTORICAL AND
LITERARY REFERENCES

Figures refer to item numbers

131

Éstoire des Engleis (Gaimar), 229, 242
Evangile aux femmes, 130, 319

Fair Annie, 274
Fairbairn, 173
Flanders, 150, 269, 282, 316, 329, 372
Floire et Blancheflor, 466
Franklin's Tale, 179, 251, 369, 404
Freud, Sigmund, 205
Frocin(e), 148

Gaimar, 229
Galeran II, count of Meulan, 172, 233, 234,
    467
Galeran de Bretagne, 222, 471
Gautier d'Arras, 226, 473
Geoffrey Plantagenet, 183
Gilbert, brother of abbess of Shaftesbury,
    113
Giraldus Cambrensis, 79, 236
Gottfried von Strassburg, 110, 148
Graelent, Lai de (Graelent Muer, Graelent
    Mor), 12, 27, 103, 123, 136, 150, 219,
    243, 266, 270, 406, 413, 420, 430, 499.
Griselda, 274
Gwent, 112
Guillaume d'Angleterre, 472
Guillaume de Dampierre, 120, 130, 150, 282,
    316, 329, 349, 372, 522
Guillaume de Dole, 222
Guillaume de Palerne, 156, 313
Guinevere, 346
Guingamor, Lai de, 17, 70, 139, 219, 224,
    243, 349, 351, 405, 413, 420, 431,
    465, 499, 506

Hasdans, Count of, 158
Heinrich von Freiberg, 403
Henri au Cort Mantel, 163, 300
Henricus Brito, 152
Henry I, 178, 384, 467
Henry II, 79, 89, 178, 182, 183, 186, 209,
    221, 349, 382, 456, 467
Henry III, 27, 120, 159, 279, 280, 281, 316,
    389
Henry of Blois, 114
Henry of Saltrey, 26, 177, 347, 455
Hereford, 233, 234, 236
Horn, Romance of, 110
Horn et Rimenhild, 324

Ianuals ljod, 14
Icarus, 164
Ille et Galeron, 226, 295, 324, 325, 352
Institutiones (Priscian), 152
Ireland, 272
Isidore of Seville, St, 84

Juan Manuel, Don, 273
Julia Strata, 112

Kardoel, 111

Lanovalus, 111
Launfal, 266, 427, 430, 500
Lai le Freine, 214, 427
Lawrence, abbot of Warden, 302
Lecheor, Lai du, 349, 361
Leicester, 467
Le Mans, 113
Lisieux, 158
Louis VII, 467
Louis VIII, 279, 280
Lug, 111

Mainet, 324
Marguerite de Flandre, 372
Marie de Boulogne, 269
Marie de Champagne, 475
Marlborough, 293
Mathilda of Boulogne, 269
Matthew de Warren, 269
Melion, Lai de, 265, 309
Metamorphoses (Ovid), 119
Meulan, 172, 233, 234
Morgen (Morgan la fée, Morgain), 111, 346,
    355
Monmouth, 236

Namnetes, 148
Nantes, 148
Newport, 112
None tresoriere, D'une, 469
Nones Preestes Tale, 367
Normandy, 280, 384
Nottingham, University of, 437

Oedipus, 164
Otto of Freising, Bishop, 152
Outillé, 113
Ovid, 414, 461